THE JESUS ESTABLISHMENT

Johannes Lehmann

THE JESUS
ESTABLISHMENT

TRANSLATED BY MARTIN EBON

DOUBLEDAY & COMPANY, INC., GARDEN CITY, NEW YORK
1974

This book was published in Germany under the title DIE JESUS
G.M.B.H. Copyright © 1972 by Econ Verlag GmbH, Wien und Dusseldorf

Library of Congress Cataloging in Publication Data

Lehmann, Johannes, 1929–
  The Jesus establishment.

Translation of Die Jesus G. m. b. H.
Bibliography: p. 211
  1. Christianity—Origin. 2. Christianity—
Essence, genius, nature. I. Title.
BR129.L39313   209
ISBN 0-385-08291-6
Library of Congress Catalog Card Number 73–81440

CONTENTS

I

GENESIS

A RELIGION IS BORN

RELIGIONS ARE constantly born, grow, and fade. Never, at any time, has man been without religion. No matter how different the various religions are, and how contradictory their aims seem at times, their function is the same, among the primitives as among Christians.

I want answers to crucial questions. I want to know how it happened that the anguished cry, "My God, my God, why hast thou forsaken me?" gave birth to a religion of salvation.

I am curious to find out how it happened that the victorious Roman Empire adopted the God of a nation that had been defeated and scattered to the winds.

I'd like to discover why a sect that hid in catacombs, whose followers were the suppressed and downtrodden, could spawn a state religion that prompted the world's rulers to see themselves as appointed by God.

I should like to understand why a faith that regarded the love of one's neighbor as the highest commandment came to wage wars and burn nonbelievers.

I'd like to ponder the fact that a tiny Jewish sect became a world religion that for a period of more than two thousand years shaped the whole world to such an extent that to us, civilization and Christianity seem virtually identical.

I want to describe how the Church was born, conquered the world, transformed faith into ideology, and thus lost its ideal.

I want to make a few factual observations that are provocative to an institution that sees itself as guardian of the unvarnished truth about that particular Rabbi Jesus—but that has grown unsure of itself and can't decide whether teachings, developed centuries ago, should give way to scientific theological insights and historical facts, or whether it remains unyielding while losing credibility.

I shall have to deal with Paul, who called himself Christ's servant, although the other apostles dismissed him as an Anti-Christ who was guilty of distortion, and I shall have to show why the Church is so reluctant to cite these early documents.

In the second part of this book I shall describe why the Church frequently turned on reformers who wanted to lead it back to its origins, condemned them as heretics, but elevated false teachers to the position of Church fathers.

After a good deal of thought, I decided to approach my subject from a psychological viewpoint. It isn't that I distrust the method of the historian, which also requires interpretation. Neither do I mistrust theology, despite ample reason to do so as it always discovers events that happen to be useful—it is, after all, the one science entirely devoted to my subject. But I really think that human needs, desires, and demands have remained the most constant factors through thousands of years; they permit relatively easy comparisons in the development of different religions. Concepts and conditions may change, but the need for happiness and salvation remains constant. Comparative psychology of religion makes one thing obvious: It shows the motives that were at work in creating a religion.

At the beginning was fear of elemental factors in nature. The god of thunder, Thor, after whom Thursday was named, was one of the nature gods who came alive in man's imagination. Eventually, man saw higher beings in all elements and natural happenings. The river god lived in the inland waters; nymphs populated the trees; earth became a mother goddess; the sun was a god; fertility and propagation grew into a cult; ritual acts and taboos were designed to influence and direct the deities by magical means.

Certain primitive religions never overcame the side-by-side existence of soul-filled inanimate things. Normally, a religion developed a specific hierarchic system. Competing nature gods are organized in a manner that reflects a group's own family or tribal organization. In manner of class order, including a king, noblemen, and subordinates, the divine heavens were arranged. The world of the Greek gods accorded such primitive nature gods as the Vulcan god Hephaistos, or the sea god Poseidon, the same level of existence as it did highly developed personified concepts such as that of the goddess of wisdom; all of them were subordinate to Zeus, god of the gods.

The ultimate evolution of the Greek "Father of the God" into the Christian "God the Father" seems a quite logical conclusion. A multiplicity of gods were combined into a few, which slowly amalgamated into a single god. This is clearly indicated in the Old Testament, where God has many names that only over a period of time merge into a single concept of God, Yahwe.

The most startling name for the single God of Moses is *Elohim,* which is a plural form and means "the Gods." It occurs in the ancient myths of Genesis, when it was simply still the "Gods" who created the world. The name *Zebaoth,* "Lord of the Heavenly Host," had its origin in a nature god or lord of the stars, and it prevailed until "Yahwe" replaced it; but because of the word's sacred nature, it could not be spoken, and so "the Lord" took its place.

The development of monotheism assumed a different concept of the world: the view that a single power was capable of creating the universe and of governing it. Primitive religions have always seen the world as divided into separate regions, ruled by individual deities. These might, in turn, owe allegiance to a single divine entity, but it was possible to deal independently with the various subgods. Monotheism greatly simplified the concept of the world: There remained only one power and basic principle, the origin of everything. This simplification assumed a high degree of human insight and abstract thinking. For the numerous and widely distributed entities that did not seem to be unified, a common denominator had to be found. Man first had to realize that the many characteristics of things and gods had a single original principle, which we came to know as God, or the Creator, the Almighty, the Divinity, according to individual preference.

The realization that the whole of the world, so impenetrable to man's mind, could be governed by one central principle, had the psychological significance that man no longer felt at the mercy of different elements of nature that had to be individually appeased. He had come to realize that thunder, lightning, and earthquakes were under the control of the same will as man himself; at last, he had a single entity to whom he could address himself.

The stories of the Old Testament illustrate how difficult it was for such a monotheistic concept to find continued acceptance. Moses, a great leadership personality, was capable of imagining such a single God who did not tolerate the existence of lesser gods, but the people kept backsliding to more primitive levels. While Moses was receiving the Ten Commandments, of which the first was, "I am the Lord thy God, thou shalt have no other gods before me," the Children of Israel were molding a golden calf at the foot of the mountain and worshiping it as a deity. Again and again, the history of the Israelites deals with the need to fend off the influence of alien gods and to appease

Yahwe because the people had been unfaithful to him. (There have been similar backslidings in Christianity, as, for instance, in the Adoration of the Virgin, but the Catholic Church has refrained from acknowledging this.)

With a God like Yahwe, one encounters logical difficulties: He is simultaneously the God of Vengeance as well as the God of Peace and Love; he creates the world in his own image, but he destroys it, as in the case of Sodom and Gomorrha; he punishes as firmly as he forgives; in other words, he is a God who cannot be defined, whose actions cannot be encompassed by logic, because he has too many contradictory characteristics. Like some of the entities in Greek mythology, Yahwe has been molded from elements of different, and sometimes contradictory, divine entities. This explains the ambivalence of such deities: They combine the characteristics of several antecedents under one name; they are simultaneously good and evil, God and Devil, and they create and destroy, all as parts of the same personality.

To steer away from such ambivalence, some religions put a dual principle in place of a single deity. They explain that the world was not created by a single principle, but grew from a battle between two contradictory forces: Good and Evil, Death and Life, Light and Darkness, Above and Below, Heaven and Earth; Christianity has not escaped the Principle of Contradiction within a Dual Deity, which apparently grew from human life experiences. The Devil, as incarnation of Evil vis-à-vis the "good Lord," had his inning in the Middle Ages, although he has not disappeared from the scene altogether.

Still, the development of a divine principle does not always testify to a religion as such; philosophy, in this area, runs parallel to theology. The philosopher is just as capable of postulating a single Creator as is the believer; he may advocate a Dualism, as did Friederich Nietzsche in his *Zarathustra*. Conversely, there are religions, such as Buddhism, that know no God.

But what—in contrast to philosophy—is the clearest indication of a religion's existence?

Comparative history of religion shows not only that religion follows specific rules of development—always according to the pervading intellectual view of the world—but also, independent of their degree of evolution, different religions follow an identical aim.

If we put aside the specific content of each faith, all of them—be they devoted to fertility, or the sun, or Yahwe—fulfill the same psychological function: They enable man to find his place somewhere in world and universe, and to make his influence felt.

The idea that Thor or Zeus are throwers of lightning does not, simply by establishing a personified god, make the laws of nature more comprehensible, any more than it prevents damage caused by lightning. Nevertheless, primitive man, ignorant of electricity in nature, believes that a particular attitude can exert a magical influence on the deity, even if it only means diverting disaster to other targets, as suggested in the prayer, "O holy St. Florian, guard my house, set the fire in my neighbor's."

Sorcery and magic are substitutes for knowledge of natural laws. They are designed to establish contact with certain forces, although the whys and wherefores tend to be obscure. The Christian God has ancient, residual characteristics of the gods of thunder; this was shown some two hundred years ago, when conservative believers resisted installation of lightning rods, arguing that it was an interference with God's plans if one were to divert the vengeance of lightning.

The nineteenth-century German philosopher Ludwig Feuerbach said in his lectures on "The Nature of Religion" that man's grave is the birthplace of the gods; that death and the question of the meaning of life were only a beginning of the quest for God. There is much truth in this idea, and the ancestor cults of other faiths support this point. Religion has, indeed, the task of answering man's basic questions about the why and wherefore of existence. In contrast to philosophy, religion does this without any act of logic or insight, but through traditional myths (such as the story of Creation), or by means of revelation (as with the Old Testament prophets), or through derivative, though unverifiable, testimonies of belief (as in the resurrection reports in the New Testament).

I am certain of one thing: Religion must do better than philosophy in giving the individual a chance to improve himself, either here or beyond. Even knowing where man comes from, where he is going, and what he is doing here is not enough to satisfy him. Although he has to submit to outside control day in and day out, man yearns to act on his own initiative. He wants to influence the coordinated system of birth, guilt, and fate; he wants to cut himself loose from predeterminism. That is why every religion, although born of fear, devotion, or awe, offers the great promise of salvation.

The roads differ, the aim is the same. Buddhism does not promise any outside help; only those who detach themselves, step by step, from the material world, from other people, from joy or suffering, can be freed from the wheel of rebirth and dissolve into Nirvana. The religion of Moses leads to God only when man links himself to his life on earth and does not forget his fellow man: A total of 613 rules and taboos on human relations must be obeyed by a Jew who aspires to a heavenly life. Islam, as much influenced by Judaism as is Christianity, promises Paradise to whoever surrenders himself to predetermined Kismet, while Christianity is based on the forgiving, equalizing grace of salvation. Gnosis knows the same salvation by man's own effort that is characteristic of Buddhism, except that it is based on an exclusive secret knowledge.

One view is common to all religion: Man's status, position,

and role, in the present world or after death, may be corrected or improved by his own efforts. This is emphasized more clearly in one religion than in another. In any event: Life has its reward.

But wherever there is a premium on faith, one has to pay certain fees: The believer who seeks to improve his personal fate through prayer, sacrifice, and manner of living must purchase it from the deity through appropriate rules and taboos. On earth, as in heaven, nothing is free. The people whom God allegedly chose when he appeared to Moses in a thorn bush imposed the most complicated dietary laws and restrictions on themselves that have ever been fixed by any religion. Not only are the Ten Commandments difficult to keep, but over six hundred rules and taboos must be observed if Yahwe is to forgive and send the Redeemer, the Messiah. The people who felt chosen by God, who addressed them through Moses and the prophets, erected the highest barriers in order to reach this God again. The ability to bend God to his will by prayer and sacrifice is achieved by a Jew under the most complicated conditions that any human being could possibly meet. No matter how ambivalent God is in his relation to him, the believer remains simultaneously God's ruler and his servant.

Just as double-edged is the meaning of the Latin word *religio*. According to Cicero, it goes back to *relegere*, meaning "conscientiously observing," while Lactantius says that its origin is *religari*, or "tied to God." Perhaps both are right, and religion is simultaneously a link with God and the observation of strict rules. That would mean religion is man's attempt, by means of self-imposed limitations, to force God to limit his own freedom of action: If man restricts himself, God must do likewise; if man makes sacrifices, God should sacrifice as well.

The biblical account of Creation contains the revealing sentence that God created man "in his own image." In other words, man was fashioned after God's example. That conveys an ancient, primitive thought. Feuerbach revived this idea when he referred to religion as a "projection of man's desires onto Heaven." The churches unjustly attacked him on this point. After all, considering the story of Creation—and after what, since then, the Church has managed to undertake—it is certainly permissible to turn the sentence around and say that man created God "in his image." The relation remains the same.

Christianity is, when all is said and done, a religion of salvation. Everybody knows that. But why has this particular religion managed to establish itself with us? Was there no further expansion of Buddhism, with its promise of self-made salvation, or the Greek understanding of the Gnosis? Why do we not put more value on our own efforts to save ourselves from "God's guilt" than an easy salvation through "grace"?

What did the Christian religion offer and deliver that enabled it specifically, and despite the obvious failures of Jesus of Nazareth, who died a most piteous death of his time, to succeed in attracting men, fascinating and inspiring them to remain true to this belief in their salvation despite all persecutions of their faith?

What, among the multiplicity of religions at that time, was Christianity's specific, perhaps now forgotten, "appeal"? And, above all, how was it possible that the intentions of this man from Nazareth could be so totally misunderstood?

2

JESUS DID NOT WANT A CHURCH

JESUS ANNOUNCED the forthcoming Kingdom of God. Instead, there came the Kingdom of the Church. It did not come at once, but it had to come because God's rule of the earth did not occur despite Jesus' forecast of its unexpected arrival in many parables. Even the Apostle Paul was so convinced of its imminence that he told the Thessalonians that some of them would see the return of "the Son of God" before their deaths.

But they all died before their hopes that this rule would appear "on Earth as it is in Heaven" were fulfilled. The dream that Jesus would be the Messiah and thus the King of Israel was destroyed. The Romans executed him as an agitator of disorder. The later hope, born of desperation, that he would at least appear with the early end of the world to "judge the living and the dead" has also not been fulfilled.

But yearning and memory remained. Thus the vain hope of the first Christians became an institution of hope for a new future, which to this day, two thousand years later, has not yet arrived. The sect of Rabbi Jesus developed into a community of believers that now has hundreds of millions of adherents.

To us, it appears as a logical and inescapable development that this "Son of God" should have conquered the world and made his imprint on our thoughts and actions. The Church teaches just that, and history documents it. After all, here was a Jewish sect, whose members were mainly poor people without influence; and yet, despite all persecutions, this sect suddenly became the state religion of the *Imperium Romanum*. Does this not prove that the Gospel with its "glad tidings" captured the human race? We take it for granted that Christianity as a world religion developed simply because there was a Christ whose teachings and life meant salvation.

But it isn't quite as self-evident as all that. Jesus was not the only "Christos" of his time ("Christos" is merely a Greek translation of the Hebrew "Messiah"), and neither was the Christian sect the only such community of its day; a great number of salvation mystiques and movements rivaled each other.

In addition, Rabbi Jesus did not have a new teaching of his own. Being a devout Jew, he wanted no more than that his people—and no one else—should be "redeemed" from the alien rule of the Roman. To this end, he advocated a life that was true to the laws, that came from the heart and was honest.

Rabbi Jesus had tried to bring about the arrival of Divine Rule through his call for a Revival. But he, the "Lord's Anointed," the Messiah, had hoped in vain. He died with the desperate cry, "My God, my God, why hast thou forsaken me?"

He did not speak of any new God, did not advocate a new road toward salvation, but only genuine devotion. He died, abandoned by God, the aim of his life nailed as a taunting phrase at the top of the Cross, "Jesus of Nazareth—King of the Jews."

It is not surprising that his name is not mentioned by a single historian of the period. There are a few meaningless lines in Tacitus and Suetonius, and by the Jewish historian Josephus in his account of the Christians, but that's all.

Nothing there of triumph or victory. His followers scattered in fear. It took quite a while before they began, cautiously, to collect their memories of this odd life, and to see it in a new and transfigured manner. The only sources on the life of Rabbi Jesus are interpretations, not objective reports.

The life of Jesus passed through two filtering systems, darkening and distorting it, before it was turned into an institution, before it became The Jesus Establishment.

The first filter was supplied by the writers of the Gospels. The four authors of the biblical reports are responsible for glossing over much that, following destruction of Jerusalem in the year 70, might have been dangerous for the newly organized sect of Jesus followers. They made sure that the dual role of the spiritual-political Redeemer, a concept within Jewish tradition, and his links with resistance groups against the Roman occupation, lost all political connotations and were presented as exclusively spiritual.

This darkening filter succeeded in making invisible all relations of Rabbi Jesus to the sect of the Essenes. These were re-established in 1947, when the famous Dead Sea Scrolls, which succeeded after some two thousand years in throwing light on the spiritual and religious origin of Jesus' teachings, were discovered.

The second filter distorted rather than darkened. It turned the Jewish preacher of penitence into the World Savior; it transformed the gifted human being into a Son of God. The man responsible for all this was Paul, born in the Greek town of Tarsus, who never laid eyes on Jesus. Paul projected his own, highly personal soul-searchings on Christ's seemingly meaningless death. He presented it as an illustration of man's basic dilemma of death, sin, expiation, and conciliation, and in doing so, falsely interpreted the teachings of Jesus. To Paul, the death of an unsuccessful Jewish Messiah became an act of divine salvation, which was valid for all mankind and could only be comprehended in faith. Offering a unique mixture of primitive blood sacrifice and Roman legalism—quite alien to Jewish tradition—he turned Rabbi Jesus into a suffering Messiah whose very blood had to be sacrificed so that God, through his Son, might conciliate himself with himself.

Understandably enough, the Church has shown little interest in clarifying or rectifying these distortions. There is, quite simply, too much at stake: the Church's own credibility, its very reasons for existing. But precisely these points are now being questioned by the great majority of Christians, although they don't quite know the factual foundations of their uneasiness.

True, even the Church did not receive the teachings of this rabbi in their unspoiled original form, and on this point it bears no responsibility. But it further changed the contradictory statements of the Bible, deleting, adding, and furnishing new interpretations.

History shows, however, that the Church later corrected and eliminated a number of errors and false interpretation that were due to circumstances at a given time. Anyone who takes the trouble to read up on the history of Church and dogma will find that there is hardly a misconception or truth that the Church did not encounter at one time or another in its long history. It has been used by heretics and saints as well as by those bent on reform and restoration. Often it is merely a matter of viewpoint whether the heretic wasn't actually saintly and the reformer engaged in restoration.

Yet, despite every correction and regardless of all efforts not to falsify openly the statements of the Bible, the Church succeeded in bringing about, in good faith, exactly the belief that suited it. At decisive points it made itself independent of historical truth and constructed various scholarly edifices that appeared to be perfectly logical and convincing, but that contained the crucial weakness that they would not survive comparison with provable fact.

Scientific theology, unless it acted as a vanguard against out-side attacks, recognized this dichotomy and pursued it. There has long been a literature, although it is difficult reading for the layman, that at times threw shockingly bright lights on the contradiction between what was intended and what actually de-veloped. But these insights have either been conveyed with hesitation in blunted form, or not at all. Often, the argument was made that the believers must not be weakened in their faith. Which prompts me to ask what kind of a faith this is that even in the view of theologians bases itself on the testi-mony of men of whom even Jesus certainly knew nothing, and who first developed their thoughts long after his death.

I wonder, too, what kind of faith this is that it has to be shielded against reality and fact, although these are supposedly its very foundations. The churches have always sought, all too easily and all too quickly, to answer questions with standard phraseology designed to strengthen the faith, and to substitute authoritarian statements for open discussions.

But who can know the truth—two thousand years later? I used to be struck by the image that truth is a circle, and that man may touch truth only where the points of his knowledge meet the rim of this circle. Geometrically speaking, at least, two tangential lines are necessary to reveal the shape of a circle, to make truth visible. What, then, is truth?

Whenever truth is being discussed, we are referred to a thoughtful passage in the Gospel according to John. At this point, the skeptical Pilate is questioning Jesus, baiting him, asking probing questions. Finally, the rabbi answers: "For this I was born, and for this I have come into the world, to bear witness to the truth. Every one who is of the truth hears my voice." And Pilate asks him, "What is truth?"

Each tangent touches the circle at only one point, and then goes off again into infinity. How many truths are there? And are there other, separate tangents that never, not even in infinity, touch or cross each other, countertruths that are mutually exclusive, although they serve to define the very same circle?

In other words, are the various Christian denominations just such tangents, in need of each other in order to make the central circle visible? But if so, should they represent themselves as being the one and only valid truth? Or, to move one step further and to express a thought that shocked me at first: What if the Church that Paul created never even touches the particular circle that Jesus had in mind?

II

FROM FAITH TO TEACHING

3

PAUL'S SWITCH

WHEN PAUL, toward the end of his life, arrived in Rome as a prisoner, he asked to see the city's leading Jews in order to explain his situation to them. They came and talked, and they finally wanted to know what his teachings were because—and this is a startling reason—"with regard to this sect, we know that everwhere it is spoken against." (Acts, 28:22)

They made another appointment, and when they saw Paul again, they brought a few others along. Until late at night, Paul explained the coming of the Kingdom of God and the role played by Rabbi Jesus. We are told that "some were convinced by what he said, while others disbelieved." (Acts, 28:24) Finally, "they disagreed among themselves, and so they departed." (Acts, 28:25)

That is the final comment on Paul's influence. A few sentences later, the report closes its account on the life of this man who for more than thirty years made his way from city to city within the vast *Imperium Romanum*, determined to proclaim the glory of someone he had seen only in a vision.

There would be a tragic touch about this disheartened note on Paul's final days if we didn't know he had used this narrow path between success and failure to create a movement that at one, almost frightening, moment might have become the one and only World Church. Certainly, Paul had to be constantly alert to guard against misunderstandings and wrong paths; over and over again, we find him warning those who have embraced the new teaching with eagerness and penitence. As Luther puts it, there is always talk of tears and fears, of suffering and sorrow. Often enough, Paul winds up in jail, is mistrusted by the Jews, is forced to flee in the dead of night, is set upon and beaten by officialdom.

This man covered nearly ten thousand miles during three journeys on foot or by boat. He never tired of describing his own experience in salvation. When he ran out of money, he probably worked as a tentmaker, although his parents had sent him from Tarsus to Jerusalem to study with the famous Pharisean law teacher Gamaliel so he might become a scribe, a rabbi.

But his life was totally changed by that experience at Damascus when, in the glittering sun of the desert, he perceived a still brighter light in the heaven. From the Hebrew "Saul" the "Prayed-for One," he changed his name to the similar-sounding Latin Paulus, "The Lesser, the Humble One." And, without suspecting it, he became the founder of a world religion.

Even Luke, who described the Apostle's life a hundred years later, could not anticipate this result. Even seventy years after the death of Rabbi Jesus, Christianity was still a sect that ran into arguments from all directions. We have no original sources, dating back to that time, that might tell us exactly what these counterarguments were. We only know from the story of the apostles that listeners in Athens made fun of the idea of the Resurrection. We also know that the new sect had the reputation of expecting an early end of the world, with the result that its followers neglected their daily duties and tended to "hang around aimlessly." Paul, too, complains about this tendency. But we don't know the details of the arguments, nothing that might deal with the teachings themselves.

We ourselves, living two thousand years later, are almost incapable of understanding just what the really new elements of those teachings were. We find it difficult to put ourselves in the shoes of those to whom all this was truly novel. To us, all of it is ancient and a matter of course, something with which we grew up and that, because of sheer habit, we hardly notice at all.

Yet what really was so new, attractive, and redeeming about this seminal religion that made it capable of outpacing other cults, mysteries, and religions with almost uncanny speed, without either force or compulsion? What was it about this teaching that we today accept without further thought—that, because of the changes and falsifications of the past centuries, may have become imperceptible—and that, despite all contradictions, still brings consolation and salvation to millions?

We can only guess. We have no proof. But we do have access to modern psychological and sociological methods that enable us, with a certain degree of probability, to arrive at specific inferences. These are the same methods that knowledgeable theologians use when they deal with non-Christian religions but are unwilling to apply to Christianity.

The psychology of religion knows that religions can only gain acceptance if they "speak from the heart" of their faithful, if these faithful are helped in their effort to find their place in the system of coordination of God and world while establishing a special relation to this God. This Supreme Being is not everywhere the same. Each nation, group, and civilization has its own image of God.

Yahwe, the God of Moses, can be clearly visualized. When the Children of Israel, twelve hundred years before Christ, left Egyptian slavery and reconquered Israel, it was the dawn of a new era for them. The slaves of the Nile became nomads who traveled with their herds through the desert toward a new, long-lost home. Hardly had they passed through the Red Sea, which devoured Pharaoh's army, when they arrived at Mount Horeb, where a new God manifested himself while the Children of Israel mourned after Egypt's old Bull cult with their golden calf. When Moses, after "forty days" brought the Ten Commandments down from the mountain, he proclaimed a new God, who in the course of Jewish history developed more and more into a national deity; he tolerated neither another God nor another people to worship him. He was a God who referred to "his" people as his "children," but who demanded that he be worshiped as the one and only God, although Egyptians, Persians, and Greeks had several gods. He was one God, who had "chosen" his people, the Israelites, by leading them back to the "promised land." After a long sojourn in the desert, the People of Israel arrived, conquered the Jericho fortress on the Dead Sea, and took possession of the country from which, in the year 70, they were once again dispossessed and exiled into many parts of the world. But Yahwe remained the God of the Chosen People, who after two thousand years—according to His promise—led them back to Israel, where they founded a state in 1948.

They never pronounce the name of Yahwe, their God of hope and consolation. He gave them strength when they were searching for the Promised Land and helped them to maintain their nationhood and uniqueness when they reconquered Palestine from other people with other faiths. He remained their hope in exile, where, at the annual Passover celebration, they recalled their exit from Egypt and pledged, "Next year in Jerusalem. . . ." For nearly two thousand years this pledge was an illusion, an incredible divine promise that for millennia had a taunting sound: "Hark, I have purified you, but not as silver, but tested you in the fiery oven of misery." At last, it became reality.

For two thousand years, these people have identified themselves with a God whom one cannot imagine and is not
permitted, as in other religions, to draw, paint, or sculpt. He
was a God of hope rather than of vengeance, as Christians
tend to view him in contrast to their God of love, although
their "Father who is in Heaven" is in reality none other than
the Yahwe of the Jews. Rabbi Jesus made it very clear that he
actually intended only to help his Jewish countrymen, and not
some foreigners. His God was "the God of our Fathers," this
Yahwe, whom the Jewish people "created" during their own history.

The moment this new sect left the narrow confines of
Judaism, it was forced to change its concept of the divine. No
Greek or Roman could make anything of a Jewish national God,
who only helped or punished one particular people.

Paul, in order to make his faith acceptable to non-Jews, had
to give this Jewish national deity, Yahwe, a "multinational"
character. He had to show a God to the Greeks who would
be real to them, whom they could understand and who could
understand them. He had to change Yahwe, the God of his
Fathers, in order to introduce Christ, Savior of the World.
The God of Paul remained one, single God as Moses had
proclaimed. Neighboring people, such as the followers of
Zarathustra or the pantheon of the Greeks, on the other hand,
knew rival and even evil gods. But Paul did not abandon
monotheism, nor did he yield on the commandment that no
one should depict this God. But he transformed the God who
had chosen the children of Israel, into the Creator of all mankind, a God who existed for everyone. True, this was also the
message of the Old Testament, and in this sense Paul did not
add anything new. But Paul changed emphasis. He ignored
the "God of the Fathers" and underlined the God of all mankind. He became, as he proudly admitted, "a Greek to the
Greeks," just as he was a Jew to the Jews.

Paul, who spoke and wrote Greek, went so far in his efforts
to be Greek that he avoided the phrase "Son of God," because
this was a term easily misunderstood in Greek, and instead
spoke of Jesus as "Ruler of the World," a concept that still lives
in the Greek Orthodox Church to this day. That Church
knows him not only as the "Savior," but also as the "Pantocrator," the "Almighty," whose stern visage stares down from the
vaults of Byzantine churches.

Paul's transformation of the concept of God is no mere psychological guess; it does not have to be reconstructed. We can
read it in Luke's version of the Gospel, and we find it in his
account of Paul's famous speech on the Areapag, the hill between the Acropolis and the Agora, Athens' marketplace. He
made this talk shortly after his dispute in Jerusalem, where the
original community addressed the non-Jewish world and
pledged to retain its link with the God of the Fathers and to
concern itself only with the Jews.

"Men of Athens," Paul said, "I perceive that in every way
you are very religious. For as I passed along, and observed the
objects of your worship, I found also an altar with this inscription: 'To an unknown god.' What therefore you worship as unknown, this I proclaim to you: The God who made the world
and everything in it, being Lord of heaven and earth, does not
live in shrines made by man, nor is he served by human hands,
as though he needed anything, since he himself gives to all
men life and breath and everything. And he made from one
every nation of men to live on all the face of the earth, having
determined allotted periods and the boundaries of their habita-
tion, that they should seek God, in the hope that they might
feel after him and find him. Yet he is not far from each one of
us, for 'in him we live and move and have our being,' as even
some of your poets have said, 'For we are indeed his offspring.' Being, then, God's offspring, we ought not to think
that the Deity is like gold or silver or stone, a representation by

the art and imagination of man. The times of ignorance God overlooked, but now he commands all men everywhere to repent because he has fixed a day on which he will judge the world in righteousness by a man whom he has appointed, and of this he has given assurance to all men by raising him from the dead."

Not a word about the Messiah, destined to free the Jews from alien rule, not a word about Yahwe, or the Crucifixion or the Son of God. Paul knew very well how to sketch the picture so as to be a Greek among Greeks. And still they laughed at him.

Luke tells us that they made fun of the Resurrection claim, but he does not mention what else Paul told them. Whatever it was, he obviously said something that did not fit the ideas of these non-Jews. In Athens as in Rome, Luke notes, some among the audience were won over by Paul while others mocked him.

At any rate, transformation of the Jewish national God into a universal Deity was only the foundation of the new religion, not the novel concept itself. Paul was not concerned with proclaiming a new God, but with a new intermediary between man and God, who had appeared to him in his Damascus vision. Paul represented his God to the Jews as Yahwe, just as he spoke to the Greeks of God as Creator of Heaven and Earth. In any case, God was unapproachably far and alone, even if the Greeks imagined him differently from the Jews. He says himself: "To the Jews I became as a Jew in order to win Jews; to those under the law I became as under the law—though not being myself under the law—that I might win those under the law. To those outside the law [meaning the non-Jews], I became as one outside the law . . . that I might win those outside the law. To the weak I became weak, that I might win the weak. I have become all things to all men, that I might by all means save some." (I Cor. 9:20–22)

The end, in this case, simply justifies the means. Paul

preached to the Jews differently from the Greeks. But he is either a fake or a hypocrite. Which God does he truly accept? The one who gave the Ten Commandments to Moses, or another? What kind of God was that, who suddenly needed an intermediary?

Did Paul proclaim only an intermediary, Christ, as the new element, or did he also herald a new God? What, to Paul, was the difference between Judaism and Christianity? What was this New Faith he proclaimed? The answer to this is contained in still another question: Why did Saul the Pharisee have a vision before he entered Damascus?

4

ON THE ROAD TO DAMASCUS

THOUGHTS AND insights don't just happen, even if one attributes them to "inspiration." Something that simply "comes to mind," as if from the outside, is actually the result of internal development. A forgotten thought that disappears into the subconscious, or a repressed event can both make their way to the surface of the human mind, transformed by intermediate time and experience. It often requires merely an accidental nudge —a casual word, a new experience, something overheard by chance or in passing—and the "forgotten" thought begins to germinate and, if it has been suppressed long enough, bursts dramatically into the open.

What Paul experienced as a vision before Damascus was just such a profound breakthrough, an experience that transformed his whole life. The triggering event was the unexpected voice, "Saul, Saul, why do you persecute me?" and "something like scales fell from his eyes." A man had changed.

We know of a number of such conversions. Augustine, the Church Father, had such an experience, and so did Martin Luther, who prompted the Reformation. Many others have experienced such redeeming "divine intervention."

To all of them, this transformation came unexpectedly, although they did not have the decisive experience without preparation, even though they were not aware of it.

We know that Luther, for example, searched unsuccessfully for years to find a merciful God. Recalling the decisive period of his conversion, he said a year before he died: "I could not bring myself to love the just God who punishes a sinner, but found myself hating him; as a monk, I lived an impeccable life, but still I felt like a sinner toward God, quite ill at ease in my conscience, and I did not dare hope that I had done enough to achieve conciliation. I was full of resentment toward God. Even if I was not guilty of secret blasphemy, then I was guilty at least of persistent grumbling. Wasn't it enough that the suffering sinner, condemned in eternity through Original Sin, found himself oppressed by all kinds of calamities through the Ten Commandments? Did God have to add still more suffering through the Gospel, which threatened us still further with his justice and anger? And so I boiled with fury within my confused conscience. . . ."

Luther felt that his picture of God was out of focus. But he couldn't adjust it. He was probably unaware that he wasn't warring against an unjust God, who punishes without mercy, but against a totally material model that ruled his life quite harshly from the beginning and with justice entirely untempered by mercy. True, Luther later complained bitterly that as a youngster he would be beaten as punishment for the smallest infraction. His mother bloodied him for every little thing, and his father once punished him so severely that he "escaped him and turned against him." But, because of traditional respect for his parents that had been instilled in him very early, Luther was probably never aware that his image of God the Father was suspiciously similar to that of his actual father. Richard Friedenthal writes in his biography, *Luther: His Life and Times*: "We may be sure that the disciplinary methods used by Luther's father, who adhered to the principle that loving a child means to chastise him severely, left their marks on the boy's soul. Defiance, one of Luther's most characteristic and fateful attributes, arose and was re-enforced early, particularly when he was punished unjustly. Early in his life, the image of the unmerciful judge, identical with a popular view of the Father in Heaven, hardened, and so did the concept of being totally at the unpredictable mercy of a force that could not be influenced by good behavior or merit. Weaker types are pushed into cringing and dull obedience; with a stronger character, forces of defiance are likely to develop. It took quite a while before these became fully developed in Martin Luther, but then they burst open with full force."

He first rebelled, at the age of twenty-two, when he was felled by a stroke of lightning. This prompted him to defy his father, enter a cloister, and become a monk. But as a monk, and later while professor of theology, he suffered from depressions while he unconsciously wrestled with the Father in God and God within the Father. He encountered the merciful God only about seven years later during a never fully clarified experience in the tower room of his house in Wittenberg. There he encountered the merciful God who, beyond any convulsive struggle for belief, offered the grace of salvation: "We now maintain that man can find justification not in good works, but by faith alone."

Luther wrote in retrospect: "I now felt totally reborn. The gates had opened; I had personally entered Paradise. The Scripture itself presented a new appearance. . . . While until then I had hated the very words 'God's justice,' these words now appeared to me as sweet and lovable above all others. Thus this passage in Paul seemed to me the appropriate gate to Paradise."

At least to Protestants, Luther's teaching that faith is the only means of salvation and not so-called dutiful justice is the "pure Gospel" that conveys the untainted, original meanings of

Scripture. The contrast between Law and Gospel provides the difference between the New and the Old Testament.

When Luther made this discovery, he was twenty-nine years old—a little younger than Paul before Damascus; both were in the same life period as the rabbi who had himself baptized in the River Jordan and experienced his call when he was thirty years of age.

Paul's conversion was unexpected, but not without preparation. There must have been something in his life, as in Luther's, that germinated in the dark and burst open so that the scales fell from his eyes. But in contrast to Luther, who often talked about his own life, and about whom we have independent accounts as well, little is known about Paul; we are limited to what sparse information may be found in his letters and what Luke reports in Acts.

"I am a Jew," we read (Acts 22:3 f.), "born in Tarsus in Cilicia, but brought up in this city [Jerusalem] at the feet of Gamaliel, educated according to the strict manner of the law of our fathers, being zealous for God as you all are this day. I persecuted [pursued] this way to the death, binding and delivering to prison both men and women, as the high priest and the whole council of elders bear me witness. From them I received letters to the brethren, and I journeyed to Damascus to take also those who were there and bring them in bonds to Jerusalem to be punished."

That is just about all we know about Saul/Paul in terms of biographical information prior to his conversion. But it is worth translating this sparse text into imaginable reality.

It must have looked something like this:

Paul probably came from a family of well-to-do traders who could afford to send a son abroad for study in Jerusalem. To begin with, Tarsus (which is today part of Turkey) was then a well-known and prosperous mercantile center that attracted many businessmen. In addition, Paul had received from his father the right to call himself a "Roman citizen." This rare privilege could only be obtained through substantial payment, as may be seen from a dialog between Paul and a suspicious Roman staff captain: "So the tribune came and said to him, 'Tell me, are you a Roman citizen?' And he said, 'Yes.' The tribune answered, 'I bought this citizenship for a large sum.' Paul said, 'But I was born a citizen.'"

Despite this account, Paul's father was not a Jew living in the Diaspora as a Roman citizen who had forgotten his Judaism and become assimilated. Tarsus, after all, had a famous university comparable to that of Athens, but Paul's father was obviously determined to send his son to faraway Jerusalem. The University of Tarsus, like the rest of the town, was permeated by Hellenic civilization.

One might compare a Jew enjoying Roman citizenship with an American Jew who, two thousand years later, lives a totally American life all through the week, but who hears the Bible read each Sabbath in his synagogue in the original Hebrew and who also contributes his tithe to the State of Israel.

It was, therefore, quite natural that young Paulus spoke Greek with the same fluency as the Aramaic of Palestine, and that he was familiar with non-Jewish cultures from childhood. Paul's father was apparently quite strict in his faith: He sent his son, probably when the boy was fourteen years old, all the way to Jerusalem just so he might go to school under the famous Jewish scholar Gamaliel. It would have been easier in Tarsus, but it was no place for Jewish orthodoxy.

In modern terms, Paulus was studying "theology," as was the case with Luther when his father sent the fourteen-year-old boy to Magdeburg to attend the school run by the "Brothers of Communal Life." Young Luther remained in this commune-type boarding school, which German Bishop Hanns Lilje in his *Luther* (1965) describes as a "Treasure of noble lay piety," adding somewhat naïvely that there can be no doubt "the fourteen-year-old boy must have come away from there with the very best impressions."

Luther's candid memories were somewhat ironic. He referred to an ascetic beggar-monk of that time thus: "To see him would prompt one to mouth-watering devotion."

We know nothing of comparative impressions on the part of Paul. We are told only that childhood memories seemed to compel him toward compensations through a particular power of faith. Luke speaks of Paul's teacher, Gamaliel, as a scholar and a member of the Supreme Council, notable for his tolerant attitude generally and toward the new sect of Rabbi Jesus in particular, a man obviously moderate in his theological views. Paul, on the other hand, was harsh and intolerant. He hunted down every deviation, including that of Jesus and his followers, crudely and with a total lack of empathy. If anyone so much as offered a different interpretation of the Torah, the Holy Writ, Paul found him guilty of being a deviationist.

When Stephen was arrested for having blasphemed the Temple and was stoned at the Temple Gate in Paul's presence, a persecution of Christians took place in which Paul took part, first in Jerusalem and later elsewhere. And there, during a moment without doubt, it happened: "Thus I journeyed to Damascus with the authority and commission of the chief priests. At midday . . . I saw on the way a light from heaven, brighter than the sun, shining around me and those who journeyed with me. And when we had fallen to the ground, I heard a voice saying to me in the Hebrew language, 'Saul, Saul, why do you persecute me? It hurts you to kick against the goads. . . .'" (Acts, 26:12–14) The word "goads" is equivalent to "spurs," as used in spurring-on a horse.

In contrast to Luther's life history, it is not possible to trace a psychological development in Paul's experience. There is no known preparation for the Damascus episode. Paul tells us of no periods of doubt that might have preceded this experience.

He does not speak of conflicts that might have directed or influenced his life. He talks about his life in disconnected segments. For him, there was a Saul prior to the Damascus conversion, and a Paul afterward. His life looks like that of a butterfly: The cocoon disappears, and the full-fledged butterfly emerges in a process of mysterious incarnation.

Such silence is curious. Converts tend to harp over and over again on the causes of their change. They reiterate their reasons, if only by painting their previous life in the darkest possible colors. Augustine did this in his *Confessions*. Luther spoke of his hate and fear. We even know more about Jesus—who did not himself write one line—his environment, family affairs, and his relationship to his mother, than we do about Paul.

In order to discover which repressed conflicts led Paul to his Damascus crisis and a new beginning, we can't search through any sort of biography and collect the kind of data psychologists accumulate, with the result that comparison with similar case histories points toward the developments that most likely may have occurred in this case. A depth psychologist, who may never have heard of Luther, could very well construct a fairly correct outline of his God image as long as he knew what Luther later told about his education and his father.

Paul seems to offer nothing like that. His is a straight, life-story line. He came from a strict Jewish family, and, by way of a rigid Jewish environment and education, arrived at a strict, almost fanatic, outlook.

This external picture would not prompt a psychologist to anticipate that this man would one day make a complete reversal. Generally speaking, Paul added up to the kind of set "type" who might simply go along as before, unchangeable and resisting all variation.

Still, just such an unexpected breakthrough of internal conflict is likely to reveal the essential, until then repressed, character. Such a return to a true personality, something not at all consciously known, is then experienced as "inspiration," as intruding from the outside. What, in this man's life, was this essential element?

After two thousand years of Christianity, we now know in general terms the conflict of Saul/Paul: the contrast between Law and Gospel as we have been "taught," which was revealed through God's guiding hand in the Damascus experience. Luke tells us in Acts 26:16–18 that Paul received a new life's task in the midst of his vision: "But rise and stand upon your feet; for I have appeared to you for this purpose, to appoint you to serve and bear witness to the things in which you have seen me and to those in which I will appear to you, delivering you from the people and from the gentiles—to whom I send you to open their eyes, that they may turn from darkness to light and from the power of Satan to God, that they may receive forgiveness of sin and a place among those who are sanctified by faith in me."

According to two other accounts of the same experience (Acts 9 and 12), Paul received these instructions later on in the city of Damascus. One of the reports places them three days later. This suggests that he had a vision that frightened him, for he did not know its meaning (if we go by these accounts), whereas Luther's tower experience created something like instant insight. In Acts 22, the same interpretation (which in 26 comes directly from Heaven) is attributed to a man, one Ananias. Paul had to have explained to him what his Damascus experience was supposed to mean.

These three reports are all conveyed by Luke, but they do not agree on essential points, although their direction is the same. But all three have one thing in common: They told Paul what he would have to do, although they did not say what he would have to abandon. He now had to side with the very man whom, up to that moment, he had been fighting so bitterly. But why? That remains unexplained. Antagonist becomes follower.

Yet not a single word provides motivation. We hear nothing of what was later to become Paulist theology.

The Bible, as is illustrated in the Gospel reports on Jesus, is a brittle record. It just doesn't care for psychological explanations or motivations. It describes destinations but is silent on approaches.

Obviously, we have to seek another road to reach Paul. So far, because their narratives are the most descriptive, I have only cited the three accounts that appear in Acts. But these are secondhand reports, written after Paul's death. They offer three versions. Only one of these can be correct, although all three may be interpretations. The only proper method would be to examine Paul's own account of his experience.

I have been turning the pages of Paul's Letters, or Epistles, which on hundreds of closely printed pages speak over and over again of death, salvation, and the Resurrection of the Christ whose "servant" he became. Paul upbraids, denounces, and urges his followers not to falter, but he himself tends to weaken; he suffers from "a thorn in the flesh," a mysterious illness that he fails to describe and that may or may not have been epilepsy; he lived through persecution, fear of death, and shipwrecks but is compelled to act as apostle, as emissary, since the blinding light of Damascus changed his path. I am searching for a description of this experience, something like Luther's or Augustine's or all the others whose lives were overturned; I am looking for the memory of this man who otherwise never tired of words, of writing, talking, and more writing.

I find it where Paul recounts the people to whom Jesus appeared after his death. First, "he appeared to Peter, then to the twelve [apostles]." Next, "to more than five hundred brethren at one time." And finally, we encounter this enigmatic sentence: "Last of all, as to one untimely born, he appeared also to me."

In the same Letter to the Corinthians, this sentence is repeated as if to reassure himself and others: "Have I not seen our Lord Jesus?" This one enigmatic sentence is all Paul has to say about the most decisive event of his life.

Why this silence?

5

SAUL'S GUILTY CONSCIENCE

IT LOOKS as if we are never going to find out just what led up to Paul's turnabout before Damascus. Paul himself did not talk about it, and Luke's account gives us no underlying reason for the Damascus experience. It is understandable, therefore, that a German Catholic encyclopedia, Herder's *Praktisches Bibellexikon*, sums it all up by saying: "Christ's call hits him so suddenly that we are unable to comprehend it either from the viewpoint of the history of religion or from that of psychology."

But I feel that this sentence is too quickly satisfied with a testimony of faith that puts its emphasis on the miraculous. I am dissatisfied, simply because divine intervention is at best only an explanation for the moment of conversion itself. It does not deal with its foundation. But everything on this earth has a reason, and every psychological development and event has its causes, even if they aren't always consciously recognized.

Perhaps we can find a clue, if not in Saul's life, then in Paul's biography. For that, we can draw on his own accounts and on those provided by Luke. It may after all be possible to add to the perspective of the blinding light in Damascus by searching the dark areas beyond it. Possibly, too, Paul's teachings and actions can provide retrospective insight into Saul's situation and later crisis.

As everyone knows, Paul turned away from the Jewish legal codes. He writes, for example: "For we hold that man is justified by faith apart from works of law" because "you have died to the law through the body of Christ," meaning that the law is no longer valid. "But now we are discharged from the law, dead to that which held us captive, so that we serve not under the old written code, but in the new life of the Spirit."

Such remarks strike us as self-evident; after all, we are not Jews. But then as now, such remarks strike Jews as heresy. Jerusalem researcher of religion Shalom Ben-Chorin says in his book *Paulus:* "Nothing in the life of the Jews and the Jewish people stands outside the law. Every imaginable situation has been covered by law, and is thus regulated. According to the sayings of the fathers, no one who is ignorant can be truly pious, because only a man who has studied the law day and night can face any situation. He knows (at least in theory) what is to be done at all times. If he doesn't know, he should ask his Rabbi, who will tell him, because there is no situation that has not been anticipated by law."

By overcoming the law, Paul abandoned the foundation of the Jewish faith. Certainly, we may sympathize with this rejection of rigidly regulated legality. Some two thousand years of Christianity have caused us to share his views, although Jesus said in his Sermon on the Mount: "Think not that I have come to abolish the law and the prophets; I have come not to abolish them but to fulfill them. For truly, I say to you, till heaven and earth pass away, not an iota, not a dot, will pass from the law until it is accomplished"—a remark that makes theologians uneasy. This is one of the points that dramatize how far Paul removed himself from the teachings of the man whose aims he allegedly proclaimed.

But our sympathy with Paul is likely to lessen once we

realize that he used the concept of "law" opportunistically. True, as a man writing in Greek, Paul could cite the Septuagint, the Greek translation of the Old Testament that has remained classic to this day; and the Septuagint uses the word *nomos* when it refers to law. But the Septuagint is, in this case, simply mistaken or, at least, inexact. It uses the word *nomos* not only to translate the Hebraic *mizwah*, which does mean law in a specific sense, but also for *torah*, which means a great deal more than simply a rigid law. Leo Trepp in *Das Judentum* (*Judaism*) writes: "Torah means 'guidance,' 'instruction,' because the Torah is more than just law; it is the epitome of all instruction, a guide for living. In its narrowest sense, the word Torah refers to the scroll of the five books of Moses, which is deposited in each synagogue. In a wider sense, Torah refers to the teachings contained in these books, as well as in all other books of sacred Hebrew scripture. But right along, the written word has been accompanied by explanatory interpretations. Part of these interpretations were later brought together in the Talmud (meaning teaching; from *lamad*, learning or teaching)."

The Torah not only contains the essential 613 commandments and taboos that every Orthodox Jew seeks to obey even today, but it also covers, as Ben-Chorin notes, "the whole complex of divine revelations to Israel," or, as Jesus put it, "the law as well as the teachings of the prophets." Ben-Chorin notes that it would be "an unnatural shrinking of the Torah concept if it were limited only to the law," adding that "Paul's use of the word created misunderstanding among his pagan listeners, as well as among Christian theologians."

Paul the Pharisee must have known the difference between the law as such and the Torah as a vessel of Jewish instruction and revelation. He must have known that the Old Testament knew the "Delight in the Law" as well as the "Yoke of the Law." But he did not differentiate between them. For him,

the Torah shrunk to the law only, and to him the law is a yoke.
By ridding himself of this yoke, he removed himself from
Judaism. No compromise was possible; it was a case of either-or.

Yet Paul achieved the impossible in doing away with the
law while, as his Letters indicate, continuing to regard himself as a law-abiding Jew. In the same Letter to the Romans in
which he explained that the law is no longer valid, he writes:
"So the law is holy, and the commandment is holy and just
and good." How can anyone honestly, within just a few lines,
insist on something so contradictory?

Apparently, his attitude toward Jewish beliefs and teachings
was ambivalent and discordant; or, which is also quite possible,
we no longer comprehend his initial viewpoint. If we assume
that he regarded the law as sacred, correct, and good, then why
did he have to overcome it? And if he does regard it as a yoke,
an unbearable burden that needs to be discarded, then why
does he say such confusing things?

What did the imprecise term "law" mean to Paul, considering that to us it is a dividing line between the religion of Moses
and Christianity? This question makes me wonder whether
Paul, at any point, talks about his relation to the law. I remember his sparse autobiographical note in Acts in which he said
that he was a Jew, born in Tarsus, educated in Jerusalem by
the distinguished Gamaliel, instructed in the law of his fathers. This is the passage that reappears in all the reconstructed
biographies of Paul because it affirms the picture we commonly
have of him. Here is a devout Jew from a pious family, who
through the grace of God disengages himself from the law of
his father in order to proclaim the Gospel to the world.

But there is still another passage, which is rarely cited as
relevant to his life. It is a short sentence, crowded out of its
context by seemingly more significant matters, but which destroys with one blow the idyllic picture of the pious Jewish
businessman of Tarsus who sends his God-fearing son Saul to

Jerusalem for religious instruction. Calmly and matter-of-factly, Paul writes in his Letter to the Romans: "I was once alive apart from the law."

In other words, Paul, or more exactly Saul, grew up—according to these few treacherous words—within a liberal household. Tarsus was certainly one of the most Hellenic cities in Asia Minor. His parents, being adaptable Jews of the Diaspora who actually obtained Roman citizenship, may not have been too particular in their observation of the Torah—assuming Paul was correct in his reminiscence that he once lived without the law, meaning not in a strict religious manner. If we assume that, as was customary, he was about fourteen years old when he went to Jerusalem, his "lawless" period must have been the time he lived with his parents.

The passage stating that Saul studied under Gamaliel comes from Luke, not Paul himself. It is actually part of an apologia that Luke formulated and that is addressed to a Jewish audience. It is certainly possible that Luke—writing years after the Apostle's death—tried to elevate the man by simply adding a reference to his schooling under Gamaliel in order to emphasize Paul's status as a scholar. We can only wonder: If Paul actually studied with Gamaliel, why didn't he mention it in his Letters? And if he was indeed a pupil of the tolerant Scholar, why did he turn with such merciless furor against the Jewish Christians? The Jewish-Christian encyclopedia *Die Bibel und die Welt* (*Bible and World*) notes that "recent criticism has raised doubts" as to whether Paul actually studied with Gamaliel. It isn't even certain that he was an ordained rabbi. We are sure of only one thing: Before his conversion, Paul was a Pharisee.

Even if one ignores the possibility that Paul did not study under Gamaliel, the picture Luke later created tends to change. Whatever happened, Paul probably did not follow the single-minded career leading from a pious home to pious passion that emerges from the standard biographies. We encounter a brief note, a short sentence, a mere afterthought that seems to have no relation to the Damascene vision; it seems, as in a dream analysis, displaced and put into an unimportant spot. And by means of decoding, a new image emerges that provides a small clue to the reality behind the façade.

Let us try our hand at a different kind of biography:

Saul's parents are wealthy Jews, well established in Tarsus, who have spent a substantial sum of money to obtain Roman citizenship in order to overcome their immigrant status, just as, later in history, Jews were baptized, to quote Heinrich Heine's sarcastic remark, to have a "ticket" into European civilization.

Paul's parents, then, paid their dues to the local synagogue, but placed no particular value in having their son educated within a strict framework toward his confirmation. They could afford to send their son to the prestigious boarding school of Gamaliel in Jerusalem rather than to the local Tarsus rabbi (always assuming some element of accuracy in the traditional biography). From one day to the next, little Saul moves from the liberal Greek atmosphere of Tarsus to that of the Holy City, site of the Temple. A new world opens up for him. Having been able to study the Torah, at best, in the Greek translation of the Septuagint, he now reads it in its Hebrew original. His fellow pupils know Hebrew probably a good deal better than he, who grew up speaking Greek. If he wants to be accepted—and later biographers picture him as short, ungainly, and fat—Paul will have to excel. In his own way, he may have followed his parents' pattern of adapting to other customs and mores—as he mentioned in his Letters later on—and this may have helped him to become accepted. The remarkable duality of his later dialectics may have had its beginning in this setting. And thus developed what, two thousand years later, Shalom Ben-Chorin described in his biography of Paul:

"Here in Jerusalem, we know this type of fanatical student from the Diaspora, although he does not come from Tarsus, but from New York or London. We find him frequently during demonstrations against peaceful car drivers on the Sabbath; he is one of those who eagerly throw stones at vehicles and drivers. These are the foreign Talmud students. In New York or London, they are unlikely to react in this manner against such a theoretical desecration of the Sabbath, but in Jerusalem they want to show that they are 150 percent Torah Jews. That is how we should imagine Saul of Tarsus, who boasted that he outdid many during his voyage through Judaism, who enthused about the law and took pleasure in the stoning of Stephen."

Saul sought, with the intolerance of the recently converted, to lead the uncompromising life of the pious. He tried to comply with the numerous and detailed commandments and taboos. At first, this must have been reassuring: Every life situation was supposed to have been regulated and anticipated, with nothing left to individual decision; all errors were theoretically impossible; and everything was in God's hands. Still, he may have grown restless when he realized that his very knowledge of all commandments and taboos made adherence difficult. Direct trust in God began to fade. If everything was ordered in accordance with the laws of Yahwe and his prophets and if one obeyed this rule, then it should be possible to lead a life that was automatically agreeable to God and free of a guilty conscience.

Saul discovered to his surprise that he was unable to achieve this goal. What should have been an aid to the pious became instead a cause for temptation. Instead of peace of mind, he developed inexplicable anxieties based on an elusive inability to come to terms with the things he most cared about. The more he tried, the less successful he was in avoiding what is known by the vague concept of "sin."

At first, Saul must have repressed these doubts by overcompensating for them through eager devotion. Intolerance is often a sign of internal insecurity; it battles most fiercely against the very aims we secretly desire but cannot admit to ourselves.

Unable to come to terms with it, he must have been dissatisfied and unhappy to the same degree that he clung to the Torah. The very garment of a life designed to please God became the strait jacket of an honest but unmanageable and convulsive faith; only the Damascus experience freed him from this self-entanglement.

In tracing this development, we are not just engaging in speculation. Years later, Paul spoke about them himself. In his Letter to the Roman community, he repeatedly described his relation to Jewish law. In passages written in dialectic and abstruse terms, he outlined the thoughts that led to his new faith. Suddenly, he offers a glimpse that leads from the life of Paul the Apostle back to the hidden life of Saul. Beyond theology and dogma, I suddenly read a fragment that is the confession of a great man:

"What then shall we say? That the law is sin? By no means! Yet, if it had not been for the law, I should not have known sin. I should not have known what it is to covet if the law had not said, 'You shall not covet.' But sin, finding opportunity in the commandment, wrought in me all kinds of covetousness. Apart from the law, sin lies dead. I was once alive apart from the law, but when the commandment came, sin revived and I died [meaning, presumably, that Paul removed himself from God]; the very commandment that promised life proved to be death for me. For sin, finding opportunity in the commandment, deceived me and it killed me. So the law is holy and the commandment is holy and just and good. Did that which is good then bring death to me? By no means! It was sin working death in me through what is good, in order that sin might be shown as sin, and through the commandment might become sinful beyond measure."

The former Saul of Tarsus speaks here of the tempting contradiction between rule and the desire for defiance. The very law that was supposed to give him life, meaning an intimacy with God, instead separates him still further from God; or, as the linguistic usage of his time would have it, brought death to him. Every law increases the temptation to violate it; every rule arouses the wish to transgress. If the Torah does not function as help and guideline but causes temptation instead, how unmerciful is this God, who prevents his creatures from moving nearer to him? Goethe, the German poet-scientist who was not a Christian, may have interpreted Paul's remarks more clearly than the Apostle himself when he wrote: "You guide him into life; you abandon him to pain; permit the poor to sink into guilt; And then you abandon him to suffering; because all guilt is paid for on this earth." Because it isn't the law as such that tortures Paul, but the imposition of guilt, which he calls "sin."

Paul wants to rid himself of sin, but he has no means for doing so. The law makes him aware of his own inability to live up to God's will, and so he suffers from the law. He feels that he is breaking an agreement. Yahwe made a pact with the People of Israel—Luther introduced the Latin word "Testament" —whereby he will help his people as long as it is faithful to him, meaning, as long as it abides by his laws. If there were to be a court case, Saul would rightly find himself judged guilty, because—at least, that is his conviction—he failed to live up to the agreement.

In desperation, he looks for a way out, a path that will lead to the tranquillity he so passionately desires. He has learned from his own example that man is incapable of achieving the absolute. No one can abide by all the laws of God; guilt is unavoidable.

And yet, Saul the Pharisee suppresses this idea and smothers it out with still more rigid adherence to the law. Still, he cannot be at ease with himself. "For I know," he writes, "that nothing good dwells within me, that is, in my flesh. I can will what is right, but I cannot do it. For I do not do the good I want, but the evil I do not want is what I do. Now if I do what I do not want, it is no longer I that do it, but the sin that dwells within me. . . . Wretched man that I am!"

Fear of the Last Judgment, an early end of the world, of a final accounting, was a vivid image at that time; and so Paul looked for an escape, and he found it in a parallel with legal proceeding: There is only one way to avoid conviction, and that is through an amnesty of grace that cancels all guilt.

Paul meets the merciful God, whom Luther fifteen hundred years later encountered in a similar situation. This is his new God: "For there are no distinctions; since all have sinned and fall short of the glory of God, they are justified by his grace as a gift, through the redemption which is Christ Jesus, whom God put forward as an expiation by his blood, to receive by faith. This was to show God's righteousness, because in his divine forbearance he has passed over former sins; it was to prove at the present time that he himself is righteous and he justifies him who has faith in Jesus. . . . For we hold that a man is justified by faith apart from works of law." (Rom. 3:23–25, 28)

Paul found his merciful God. But one might just as well say that he invented him.

6

PAUL FINDS A WAY OUT

PAUL TOOK over Christianity like a conqueror. He did not care what it really was, but only how he could use it. He wanted and needed a merciful God. He was like Jacob, of whom a mysterious Old Testament story says that he wrestled with God to make him do his bidding: "I will not let you go unless you bless me." Because he faltered before the law and felt himself guilty—as, later, did Martin Luther—Paul sought forgiveness and release from the guilt of his shortcomings.

He found both where his ancestors had always looked for them: with Yahwe. The God of the Old Testament, despite the version preferred by Christianity, is not just the God of vengeance who demands an eye for an eye and a tooth for a tooth. The number of times the word "vengeance" is linked to Yahwe in the Old Testament can be counted on the fingers of one hand; the words "grace" and "mercy" appear more than fifty times, which is ten times more frequently than in the writings of the four Gospel authors of the New Testament put together.

But this Old Testament mercy, which Yahwe offered his people as well as individual fathers and forefathers—meaning that Yahwe accepted them and remained loyal to them—was not enough for Paul. Such general assurance was not specific enough for him. He needed to find forgiveness for his own personal guilt. Somebody had to tell him, as did Jesus, "Your sins are forgiven." (Luke 7:48)

But Jesus was dead; still, he had asked Paul at Damascus, "Why do you persecute me?" Therefore he must be alive, "raised from the dead."

That was Paul's conclusion. And that would also be the conclusion today of anyone who does not know how real and convincing hallucinations and visions can be, although they are projected outward by man's unconscious. For decades, psychology and psychiatry have accumulated material along these lines that might save theologians from all-too-easy and all-too-believing statements. One thing is sure: Paul's personality cannot be viewed exclusively from a theological viewpoint. Many a particularly sensitive outsider has, throughout history, displayed the kind of antenna that seemed to register the good and evil forces that millions could neither express nor consciously register.

To Paul, at any rate, the appearance of the Crucified on the road to Damascus was as much a reality as Yahwe's promise to free his People. Now, Paul linked both elements in a peculiar manner. To him, Jesus suddenly became the intermediary of that particular mercy, a concept that could not have occurred to an orthodox Jew. To the Jews, Yahwe was and remains the one and only God, the God who made a pact with his People. Yahwe did not really need any form of intercession. He had always been capable of making his laws understandable to the Jewish people, and he had always, until then, been able to assure this people of his mercy, of his understanding forgiveness.

True, occasionally Yahwe had adjusted his Creation for the sake of a single human being. This tendency is illustrated in the Old Testament by the ancient story of the Flood: Because

Noah was pious and God-fearing, he, and with him mankind, were saved from destruction. But Noah was no intermediary. Noah, unlike Paul's Christ, was not a path to God.

And that is decisive: Paul erects a wall of separation between himself and God, something unknown to the Jews (but which the Catholic Church, with its interceding saints, developed still further). Paul finds only, or for the first time, access to God through Christ.

With that, Paul crushed the impressive idea, born in the solitude of the desert, that there is only one God and Creator, only one who looks after his Children like a father and in his unattainable nature remains near enough to know each one of them.

Perhaps this had to happen. It is, after all, difficult to venerate something unimaginable. The sins of the Children of Israel—beginning with the golden calf—tended to be the adoration of pagan images, visible symbols of the Invisible. But while the Jews always returned to monotheism as the highest and certainly most demanding form of divine worship, Paul surrendered: To him, the laws of God had become not a path but an obstacle.

Paul simplified the difficult faith with its demand to follow fixed rules; he depends on mercy, which erases all errors as long as one believes in it. He cannot himself testify in his defense before the Last Judgment, and so he brings along a guarantor who takes all his guilt upon himself—much like the scapegoat which, in Mosaic ritual, takes the sins of the people upon itself and is driven into the desert where, as a substitute for the others, it will perish. This concept, the outgrowth of an archaic type of sacrifice, Paul revived with his idea of "the Lamb of God" simply to be rid of his own guilt feelings.

None of this is Jewish, and certainly not in accordance with the teachings of Jesus.

Not one of the four Gospel authors offers even a single passage that quotes Jesus as speaking of mercy. He is concerned with totally different things, such as revival and fulfillment, and the coming Kingdom of God. He said that God would forgive our debts, just as we should forgive our own debtors. But Paul changed this into something quite different. In his Letters in the New Testament, which tend to interpret Jesus rather than cite him, he speaks twenty-eight times of mercy. The writers of the Gospel just as often refer to the concept of "Christ," by which they meant the Messiah. But the Letters of the New Testament speak more than two hundred times of "Christos" in the heightened, theological meaning of the word.

There is a gap between the Gospels and the Letters of Paul. Jesus did not see himself as mediator, but as a preacher of penitence. He called for a return, because God's judgment was near. He may have considered himself a Messiah, the Savior of his nation from foreign domination and as the coming "King of the Jews," but he did not regard himself as the Redeemer of personal religious doubts or feelings of guilt. Most certainly he did not see himself as the "Son of God," as part of a Trinity, to which he was elevated by later worship and the misconceptions of a foreign cultural pattern. Above all, it could not have occurred to Jesus to consider his own death as a means for the redemption of mankind and for its conciliation with God. He expected the Kingdom of God in his own lifetime; that is why he called for penitence and readiness, and had himself baptized so that his sins might be forgiven.

How, then, did the Pharisee and Jew Paul arrive at his revision of ideas, which in the end amounted to falsification of the original meaning? He did not get these ideas from Judaism. Paul does mention, in his Letters, some of the views of the first Church Fathers, but only in passing. But he was the first to turn these concepts into formal teachings and into a theology of his own. At the very least, this departure from Jewish law, resulting in a totally different view of God and the so-called

"Christology," are entirely Paul's doing. Even when Jesus is cited now and then, mentioning that the Sabbath exists for man and not man for the Sabbath, this is certainly not evidence of any intention to dissociate himself from the Law. Such interpretations have been made to excuse Paul, but it might just as well mean that Jesus wanted to return to the original meaning of the Sabbath as a way of serving God, just as he healed the sick to make them aware of God. He was against rigid ritualization of the Law, but he did not favor its dissolution, as advocated by Paul, who wanted to be a Jew to the Jews and a Greek to the Greeks.

Paul was entirely too iridescent a personality to fit neatly into one category or another; he was all things to all men. By origin, tradition, and education he was a Jew, but in his teachings and actions he was a non-Jew.

He stands revealed in his Letters. Paul used the traditional in order to communicate the novel; he used a new approach in order to convey the traditional. He changed the old and transported it into his own world, which is the world of Hellenism. As a result, his ideas add up to a synthesis of Judaism and Hellenism. Even he could no longer tell where one ended and the other began, whether the Old was more important than the New, or the New more important than the Old.

Saul/Paul stood between two worlds. He had grown up in the Greek city of Tarsus and received his strict education in Jerusalem. But he did not have deep roots in either place. He was dissatisfied with the ideas represented by the two most formative forces in his life. It took him years to combine the extremes that had molded him. The breakdown at Damascus solved his repression. The result was a synthesis of the Jew Saul and the Roman citizen Paul. His teachings became a mixture of Jewish belief, Greek philosophy, and of the yearning for salvation embodied in Eastern mystery cults.

Erwin Jaeckle writes in *Die Osterkirche* (*The Easter*

Church, 1970) that Paul's great achievement in the history of religion was "a fruitful marriage" of ethics, mysticism, and eschatology [the teaching of ultimate things, referring specifically to the expected Kingdom of God]. Jaeckle says that Paul "Christianized the Platonic design by letting God enter the world's suffering. Christ 'becomes sin.' . . . The Paulist concept was as much Greek as Christian. It was Platonic in the sense that it spoke of God's Image, man's duality, and the rise and fall of everything that is of the earth."

Similarly, Carl Schneider observes in *Geistesgeschichte der Christlichen Antike (A History of Ideas in Christian Antiquity,* 1970): "Paul not only poured the Christian concept of charity into a Greek mold, but he followed the path of the 'Hellenists' with consistency. To him, the Christian experience permits ready entrance into the world of the mysteries, particularly that of Hellenistic religious philosophy. . . .

"At the base of all Platonism lies this pattern: Idea, Image, and World of the Empirical. These became the pattern of Paulist thought, although with stronger religious significance. Within all of philosophy and religion influenced by Plato, we can find a constantly fluid relation between the downward-moving Heavenly and the upward-moving Earthly."

The static confrontation between God and Man, Creator and the Created, which Jewish thought defined and regarded as beyond intermingling, was turned by Paul into a mystical interchange. In Genesis, the snake says, "You will be like God, knowing good and evil." It was this that led to Man being driven out of Paradise. By contrast, Paul sees the upper world as permeating the lower one: God may become Man, and Man may become God.

Paul perceives the Divine only "as in a glass darkly," just as Plato, in his analogy of the caves, observes "ideas" only in shadowy outlines. But Paul also says that only those can know God who have already become infused by God. Within the unspeakable secret of this mysticism, such insight results from an essential interchange: "Now that you have come to know God, or rather to be known by God." (Gal. 4:9).

Just as at Damascus he did not encounter a Jewish Messiah but a Hellenistic Son of God who "sits at the right side of the Lord," Paul turns the man Jesus into a mystical experience. In his Letter to the Galatians he advances the thought that he lived in Christ and Christ within him; objectively, this is a dialectical expression, but as an experience it is mystical.

Paul reaches the pinnacle of his spiritual mysticism when he unites Christ's suffering with man's suffering in his search for God. Schneider maintains that Paul extracted the concept of this mystique from "the compassion of the mystics with the suffering God in the mystery religions." Paul, according to Schneider, went beyond this: "Only the fact that the bearer of the spiritual burden shares his Lord's suffering manifold, proves that both are united in spirit: 'We carry the death of Jesus within our person at all times, so that the life of Jesus may be revealed to us.' This joint suffering is thus a constant part of the person's existence, something that permeates his whole life. It was Paul's supreme pride to be able to say, 'I bear the wounds of Christ on my person,' or 'the sufferings of Christ have increased vastly with us.' It can even come to the point where the spiritual bearer senses a need to complete Christ's burden by way of his own suffering: In other words, Christ did not suffer enough to bring God's Plan of Charity into being, and therefore the suffering of both must become one."

Here, then—far away from Judaism and the teachings of Jesus—is the core of the much-misunderstood Christian willingness to suffer. Later influences deepened it still more, divesting it of its mystical background and culminating in the theory of a Valley of Lamentation, totally lacking in any Christian reality, which wanted only to bear the Cross and meet everything with passivity. But Paul should not be held responsible for this later development. For him, within the Platonic example, Christ is the vessel of God's essence. That is the image he pursued. In doing so, he transformed Jewish thought into the "universality" of his contemporary Hellenic world, and changed it profoundly.

While John the Baptist washed human sin away in the waters of the River Jordan, Paul turned baptism—as in the mysterium of Osiris, where the child is drowned with Osiris—into direct participation in Christ's suffering: "And you were buried with him in baptism, in which you were also raised with him." (Col. 2:12)

The Jewish Seder, the meal at the Passover feast, becomes a memorial feast in the sense of Platonic recall, a form of anamnesis, whose essential meaning does not lie in mere repetition of the Lord's Supper but in a questioning remembering of the "idea" of the essential, of God, oddly mixed with mystical participation in a repeated sacrifice.

The ancient Greek concept that the fury of a God could be appeased by human sacrifice—Iphigenia had to be sacrificed on Aulus so the angry gods would send favorable winds for the sea voyage to Troy—is combined with the Old Testament story of Isaac's sacrifice. But in both cases the message is clear: No longer, as in olden times, does God desire human sacrifice. In both cases, divine intervention substitutes an animal for the human victim.

Paul, the mystic, turns the whole thing around. He once again places a human sacrifice in the position of the Lamb of God, which had been sacrificed in Jewish ceremonies. Here, too, he goes counter to the actions and thoughts of Judaism. Paul now teaches that to conciliate God, a human sacrifice must be made. God himself had to appear as a servant, demean himself, so that death be subjugated by death, and God might conciliate himself with himself.

To advance this new teaching, Paul had to change the God

image of Yahwe. He could no longer be the God who permitted himself to be appeased by the deeds of his creatures as the law had defined them. To a Jew, piety could only be measured in deeds. Paul's God followed the pattern of deities known from the mysteries of salvation.

With all this, Paul managed to gain mercy through his curious mixture of Greek mysticism and Roman legalism. He who wanted to be a Jew among Jews found salvation among the Greeks because he was a Greek among Greeks. To achieve this, he turned them into the followers of a Jew who had perished at the Cross. It was Jesus' death, not his life, that absorbed their interest.

Only death, not life, mattered in the mysterium of divine sacrifice. Paul therefore was not interested in the historical Jesus. He did not need him. But his death at the Cross, which summed up Jesus' failure—"My God, my God, why hast thou forsaken me?"—became salvation and thus victory through Paul.

Paul could not find salvation in the teachings of Jesus, who had been a law-abiding Jew, who did not come to dissolve the law but to envigorate it by his humanity. Paul, who had found the law wanting, found it easy to forget Jesus' intentions and to turn his failure into the victory of a new idea. Yet it was an idea that Jesus had not known. If he had known it, he would have rejected it as blasphemous; and not only he.

7

A CERTAIN "HOSTILE PERSON"

WE DO NOT know why Paul picked Jesus, specifically, to say something novel. But even more mysterious is the role of the original community of Christians in Jerusalem. Why did they, who had known Jesus personally, accept Paul's reinterpretation? Were they in such despair about the absence of the Messiah and the Kingdom of God that, against their own better judgment and at the cost of falsification, they agreed to Paul's teaching? These were men such as the Apostle Peter, and Jacob, Jesus' brother. What could prompt them to such a 180-degree turnabout? Wouldn't it have been more honest if they had said, like others before and after them, that this one, too, was not our promised Savior?

We know very little about this original community, and what we know is told by Luke, who may well have accompanied Paul on his journeys, and, of course, by Paul himself. Both were mainly concerned with widening the influence of their sect. When they do speak of Jerusalem, it is often only to report disagreements between Paul and Peter.

At any rate, this picture emerges. Seven weeks after Jesus' death, when all Jews celebrate Shavuoth in memory of the Ten Commandments, the Apostles in Jerusalem had a mystical experience, which the Gospel calls an outpouring of the Holy Spirit. The Apostles are obviously engaged in enlisting new followers. Like John the Baptist, they call for repentance. In the manner of the Essenes, the small group operated on a communal basis. Luke reports: "And all who believed were together and had all things in common; and they sold their possessions and goods and distributed them to all, as any had need. And day by day, attending the temple together and breaking bread in their homes, they partook of food with glad and generous hearts."

Luke also writes that the community was beloved by everyone, but that was simply not true. On the Shavuoth day they were treated as drunks, and as soon as they started to talk about Jesus they came into conflict with Temple officials and the captain of the Temple.

The new sect was forced to develop its own hierarchy parallel to that of the Temple. With Peter as their leader, the twelve Apostles formed the nucleus of this organization. To serve in their welfare work, seven deacons were named. One of them, Stephen, was stoned to death soon afterward.

The workings of this "Supreme Council" show that it acted as a sort of counterrégime to the Sanhedrin, which was then the highest Jewish authority. The Sanhedrin, known from the Bible as the "High Council," was made up of seventy-one members who raised Temple taxes and guarded the observance of religious laws in Jerusalem as well as abroad. The High Council was the final court of appeal for questions concerning adherence to the law, the Torah.

Similar functions were exercised by the "Supreme Council" of the Jerusalem community. Hugh H. Schonfield summarizes them in *These Incredible Christians:* "They send out officers to supervise new communities of believers, Peter and John to Samaria, Barnabas to Antioch. They dispatch, with the president's commission, a delegation to Antioch to investigate the terms of admission of Gentile converts, and when there is a dispute on this matter the case is referred back to Jerusalem for final decision, and James the president gives judgment. The interference with his work and teaching which Paul so much resented was action mandated to its official representatives by the Christian Sanhedrin in accordance with its supreme authority and in due performance of its obligations. . . . Further, in the Acts and Pauline writings, we find a practice of collecting funds among the communities and transmitting them to Jerusalem, comparable to the payment of the Temple tax by Jews of the Dispersion."

It was this governing body of Jews, motivated by loyalty to their Messiah, that Paul had to confront during his second visit to Jerusalem.

His first visit had taken place three years after his conversion at Damascus. "And when he came to Jerusalem," Luke writes, "he attempted to join the disciples; and they were all afraid of him, for they did not believe that he was a disciple. But Barnabas took him, and brought him to the apostles." (Acts, 9:26–27) Barnabas had to report in detail on Paul's change of view before he even got as far as to talk to the Apostles. Nevertheless, the first visit ended in discord: Paul quarreled with the original community and fled Jerusalem because its members planned to kill him. Those are the details we learn from the Gospel account.

In his Letter to the Galatians, Paul totally ignores the distrust he encounters as well as the quarrel. "Then, after three years," he writes, "I went up to Jerusalem to visit Cephas [Peter], and remained fifteen days. But I saw none of the other apostles, except James [Jacob], the Lord's brother. In what I am writing to you, before God, I do not lie!" (Gal. 1:18–20)

Why, at this apparently quite uncontroversial point, does Paul feel prompted to swear that he is not lying? At the very least, he must have sought to contradict widespread rumors. In reality they were not merely rumors.

It seems that, from the very beginning, Paul's relations with the Jerusalem community were uneasy. None of the reports suggest that his first visit led to an agreement concerning teachings. Presumably, Paul accomplished a good deal by not being thrown out as a spy. After all, he had only shortly before participated in the stoning of Stephen, and his extreme hatred of the Christians had led to his appointment as emissary to Damascus, where he was supposed to deal with other followers of the sect. But there was trouble even during his first Jerusalem visit. After Paul's hasty departure, Luke comments naïvely: "So the church throughout all Judea and Galilee and Samaria had peace. . . ."

It took another fourteen years before Paul returned to Jerusalem for a second time since his conversion, and even this was under pressure. All this time, Paul, together with Barnabas, had been on a missionary campaign in the Antioch region of Syria. In the seventeen years since his conversion, he had never come to a meeting of minds with the Jerusalem community. In the meantime, he had abandoned circumcision, which for all Jews, as well as for the first Christians, had been an essential rite. His teachings on the Cross and Jesus' act of salvation, which had nothing to do with Christ's actual life or death, had also been developed.

That Paul visited Jerusalem at all was due to a divine "Revelation." (Gal. 2:2) The Gospels speak of no such revelation. In matter-of-fact phrases, they note that a traveling delegation from Jerusalem had found out that Paul had given up circumcision, and had quarreled with him about it. As Paul refused to give in, he was asked to appear before the High Council of the original community in Jerusalem and confront the Apostles.

The relevant passage reads as follows: "But some men came

down from Judea and were teaching the brethren, 'Unless you are circumcised according to the custom of Moses, you cannot be saved.' And when Paul and Barnabas had no small dissension and debate with them, Paul and Barnabas and some of the others were appointed to go up to Jerusalem to the apostles and the elders about this question." (Acts 15:1–2)

In other words, the Jerusalem community was not at all in agreement with Paul's teaching. What the Church later called an "Apostolic Concilium" was nothing but a tribunal before which Paul had to defend himself against accusations of spreading false teachings.

Paul had to confront the council, and soon there was another quarrel. Even Luke admits that there "had been much debate."

According to Luke, a compromise was worked out. Paul recalled later that Peter, Jacob, and John agreed to do missionary work among the Jews, while he and Barnabas restricted themselves to the non-Jews.

Christian interpreters, embarrassed by this quarrel among their spiritual ancestors, have maintained that Paul was in the right but that his passionate, quick-tempered personality got the better of him when he confronted the short-sighted Jewish Christians. This view gains credence from the fact that Paul had another run-in with Peter shortly after the Apostolic Concilium and soon afterward he also quarreled with his longtime companion, Barnabas, about something quite trivial, which led to a breakup of the two men.

But Luke may just as well have been trying to camouflage a final break between Paul and Peter. Or maybe Paul had another memory lapse like the one he had had before, when he attributed to divine revelation the reason for his quite down-to-earth and painful appearance before the Jerusalem tribunal. We might also consider that division of the world between Jews and pagans may only have meant that the Jews who were loyal to their Messiah wanted the troublemaker out of their realm. He did, after all, talk about things the Apostles had witnessed. To them, who called themselves "Christians" after the Jewish "Messiah," it could have mattered little what happened to the pagans who had crucified him. But we can leave this matter an open question.

It is certainly odd that Paul, when he visited Jerusalem for a third time, toward the end of his life, was forced once again to defend himself against charges that he was teaching defection from the law of Moses. When he was recognized by Jews from Asia Minor, there was an altercation in the Temple: "Men of Israel, help! This is the man who is teaching men everywhere against the people and the law and this place. . . ." (Acts 21:28) Paul was arrested and imprisoned for two years before being taken to Rome. But not once do the Gospel accounts mention even one attempt by the original community to contact Paul, to help him, or even to have him freed during those two years. And this despite the fact that Luke devotes eight of twenty-eight chapters in the Acts to Paul's imprisonment.

Luke reports that Felix, the Roman governor, had given instructions that Paul should not be kept in strict custody, and that "none of his friends should be prevented from attending to his needs." (Acts 24:23) But in the whole account of his prison years, we read about only one of Paul's "friends" who interceded for him. And he was not a member of the Jerusalem community but a blood relation, somebody who is not mentioned in any biography of Paul. Still, this visitor is of some interest, possibly even significance, because he shows that the Diaspora Jew Paul had relatives in Jerusalem. He is a nephew, "the son of Paul's sister," who hears of a plot against his uncle and goes directly to the prisoner to warn him. He is the only one who cares about Paul. Then Paul is taken to Rome, where he meets death.

That is about all that is known of Paul's relationship to the

Jerusalem community. Nowhere is there a report that the community endorsed Paul's views. At the very most, if we follow Luke's accounts, it permitted Paul to go his own way. Luke usually states that others take Paul's side in Jerusalem, report his successes, and tip the scales. Everywhere, Paul is the spellbinding speaker—but not before the community in Jerusalem. There he is on the defensive. Once Paul even writes proudly that he didn't knuckle down in Jerusalem. (Gal. 2:5)

It is, therefore, quite possible that the Gospel versions, not to mention Paul's own accounts, seek to sugar-coat a few points. Some disputes are reported—and there was always trouble when Paul went to Jerusalem—but Paul is always pictured as victorious. According to these reports, he was respected.

Now, we must remember that the Gospels were written between the years 90 and 100, or about forty years after the death of Paul and more than twenty years after the destruction of Jerusalem. It is not at all unlikely that the judgment on Paul had undergone a change during the intervening years. No original community in Jerusalem, not one of Jesus' disciples, could speak up against any distortion of history. All of them had left Jerusalem about the year 66, at the beginning of the Jewish War. They settled in Pella, about the level of the Sea of Genezareth, east of the River Jordan in non-Jewish territory.

The Gospel reports are certainly weighed in favor of Paul. We can see this clearly from the fact that the fate of the Jerusalem community is only mentioned when some event connected with it tends to underline Paul's influence. That the Jerusalem community, and with it Jesus' immediate relatives as well as the still-living disciples, migrated to Pella is not even hinted at. The Gospel texts are silent on the fate of those who had seen it all with their own eyes. The impression is created that, with the destruction of Jerusalem, the Jewish-Christian group had been eliminated.

The Church Fathers Epiphanius, Theodore of Cyrus, and others note that descendants of the Jerusalem community lived in Syria down to the fourth and fifth century. After that, probably because of internal disputes, all evidence of them is lost. They called themselves "Ebionites," which means "the poor," because their ancestors in Jerusalem had lived in common poverty as part of their faith. These were the true inheritors of the first disciples and brothers of Jesus, of the people who had known him, knew what he thought, wanted, and did; they knew what he looked like, and their hopes were built on him—until they disappeared in the mountains of the Jordan desert without leaving a trace in the history of the Church.

Eusebius, one of the Fathers of the Church, states that, after Jacob met a martyr's death in Jerusalem, another relative of Jesus became head of the Pella community. He was Simeon, son of Clopas. Several members of Jesus' family are said to have succeeded him in his bishop's office at Pella. All this faded into a silence beyond history.

Still and all, the Roman Catholic Church did not forget the Ebionites. It did not elevate them to sainthood, as one might well have assumed; rather, in the second century the relatives of Rabbi Jesus were declared *haeresis soleratissima*, members Schoeps, writing in *Theologie und Geschichte des Judentums* of a particularly despicable sect. According to Hans-Joachim (*Theology and History of Judaism*), "The growing Greater Church officially turned against these isolated special groups which had abandoned all contact with the missionary groups in the pagan Diaspora in favor of their essential Judaism, and in the course of the second century declared them to be heretical." Schoeps, speaking of the Ebionite group, writes that "its personal and spiritual relation to the Jerusalem community is not in doubt."

Heresy. It seems unimaginable, and one asks why. These were the people who created the High Council of Christians in Jerusalem in the year 66; they were the Loyalists of Christ, the Messiah who guarded the law and who took martyrdom upon himself; they were part of a tradition that they knew not from hearsay, but direct participation, and these were the people who were condemned as heretics. Why?

Unfortunately, we must rely on very few sources to seek fragments of the truth. We know that the Ebionites had their own Gospel, a life story of Jesus that showed considerable similarity to the Gospel according to Matthew. But the full text of the Ebionite Gospel has been lost. We only know excerpts from the writings of Epiphanios of Salamis, who lived in the fourth century and reported on the Ebionites. They also appear to have their own apostolic records. Remnants of these documents may be found in the so-called pseudoclementic novel, an epic narrative to which Christian elements were added in succeeding later versions. On the assumption that significant elements may have been retained even in such a secondhand source, some useful data may be elicited from this material.

We learn from it that the Ebionites were particularly law-abiding Jew-Christians. They observed the Sabbath, engaged in specific ritual purifications, were critical of Old Testament canons, and had their own Christ teachings, so that their relationship to the Essenes of the Dead Sea is not only based on a common poverty ideal. That alone would not have branded them as heretics. What was decisive was their refuge in Trans-Jordan, which served to cut them off from dogmatic developments elsewhere; it prompted them to deny the later concept of the Virgin Birth (as relatives of Jesus, the Ebionites must have known something about this). They also knew nothing about the divine conception of the man of Nazareth, but favored the biblical version whereby union with the Holy Spirit took place during the baptism in the Jordan when God's spirit lowered itself to Jesus "like a dove."

All this could be regarded as heresy by the evolving Western church, as a deviation from correct teachings, although the divinity of Christ remained embattled for centuries before it was raised to the level of dogma. But it still does not explain why the Ebionites should have been labeled as "particularly repugnant heretics."

The reason for this is easy to find, although even recent Catholic works carefully avoid any mention of it. The Ebionites were battling a particular antagonist, whom they called a "hostile person." This enemy, whom they also described as a "pseudo apostle" and "Anti-Christ," had once attempted a murderous attack on Jacob, chairman of the Jerusalem community, by deliberately pushing him from the top of the Temple stairs. Jesus' brother barely escaped death.

According to the Ebionites, this event took place at Easter of the seventh year following Jesus' death. The occasion was a sort of general meeting of the original community, organized as a discussion by the Jewish priests as to whether or not Jesus had been the Messiah promised by Moses.

Other passages show clearly that this "hostile person" and "pseudo apostle" was none other than Paul of Tarsus, who appears in a rather dubious light even in the Gospel accounts endorsed by Christianity.

Even the time element could be correct. The stoning of Stephen, through which Saul/Paul caused the first persecution of the Christians, happened about three years after Jesus' death. Paul then had his vision near Damascus, and it took another three years before he returned to Jerusalem for the first time. It was precisely seven years since Jesus' death.

Let us look back, once more, to Paul's own account of his visit to Jerusalem, when he stayed with Peter. He wrote that he spent fifteen days with him, "saw no other apostles except James [Jacob], the Lord's brother." And he added: "In what I am writing to you, before God, I do not lie!"

Paul invoked the name of God in an oath that would seem to deal with only a relatively unimportant matter. Of course, he met Jacob. But aren't gaps often the most important factors in a biography? The things people skip in their life stories are often the most intimately decisive. Who, after all, likes to admit his own guilt? And why does Paul have to fall back on a divine vision that urges him, "Make haste and get quickly out of Jerusalem, because they will not accept your testimony of me. . . . Depart for I will send you far away to the Gentiles." (Acts 22:18–21)

Seventeen years later, Paul transformed another external force into a divine command, when ordered to appear before the so-called Apostolic Concilium in Jerusalem.

And does not the short sentence saying he is sent "far away" among the pagans reveal clearly that the Jerusalem community could not accept his teaching and was ready to be rid of him, while he was willing to go where no one would interfere with him?

The Pseudoclementine text contains an argument between Peter and Paul, which dramatizes the unbridgeable gap between the Jerusalem community and the "pseudo-Apostle" in detail. Peter tells Paul: "If Jesus appeared to you in visions, then only as Jesus presents himself in anger to his antagonists. How can anyone receive instructions for teachings by way of a vision? And if you answer that it is possible, then why did the Master communicate with us in our waking state? Why should we believe you at all when you claim that he appeared before you? And how could he appear to you, when you believe the very opposite of his teachings? . . . If you really wish to serve the truth, then first of all learn from us what we have learned from Jesus."

The Church declared the Ebionite eyewitnesses to be heretics because they doubted the main witness of the growing Church, Paul the visionary. Yet it wasn't the Jerusalem community that reversed the teachings of Jesus by 180 degrees, but the self-appointed Apostle Paul, who turned the call for penitence of a Jewish rabbi into an extra-Jewish religion. The actual descendants of the man of Nazareth, the Ebionites, disappeared, and with them their teachings. The victor was the man whom they would not recognize: Paul of Tarsus. What made his teaching so attractive that it became a world religion?

III

FROM TEACHING TO CHURCH

8

SALVATION ON CREDIT

WE MUST remind ourselves over and over again that Paul was only a minor traveling preacher. True, with prophetic impatience he moved from town to town, proclaiming a new faith. But in his time he was only one of thousands who appeared as teachers and prophets to offer salvation.

The Greek Pantheon had grown old and tired. Various sects and mystery cults had begun to spring up. The need for salvation was particularly strong with common people and slaves, all those to whom life on earth had little promise. Johannes Gaitanides writes in *Inseln der Agais* (*Islands of the Aegean*): "The Eastern gods of Salvation that could be found on its coasts were finding new and fertile ground on the islands of the Aegean Sea; they were such gods as Isis, Sarapis and Mithras." He notes that "on the same wave, Christianity poured over the hellenistically-oriented world. Certainly, the Christian God did not strike down on these areas like sudden lightning, as something totally different and new, something that might have bridged a yawning gap of irreconcilable differences, something unconnected to all of preceding history."

True enough, what Paul had to offer was not essentially new. Salvation was the key concept of the period. No one had to fall back on the odd story that a Jewish national God had permitted his "Son" to be nailed to a cross, like a criminal, in order to achieve mankind's salvation.

Still, there had to be something that lifted Paul's teaching above all others. Somewhere Paul must have touched a deep and universal need that convinced people to share their fate with the Christ. But before searching for this unique element, I want to compare the new teaching with competing mysteries and cults. Of course, one Roman Catholic specialist of the New Testament, Rudolf Schnackenberg, writes in *Der frühe Gnostizismus* (*Early Gnosticism*): "There is considerable disagreement as to the influence which Gnostic themes may have had on Christianity when it made its early appearance in the hellenistic setting, or even on the development of Christology itself. It is doubtful that the so-called Gnostic Salvation Myth was essential to the Christology of the Early Church, particularly in the light of recent research in the history of religion."

But in this case, as elsewhere, such statements are no more than the conclusions expressed by a single theologian, who is able to discover in his sources exactly what he has been looking for; it certainly does not reflect the general theological view, and most certainly not the opinion of the appropriate special discipline of the history of human thought. Anyone who is even slightly familiar with the literature of theology knows very well that it hardly ever deals with a situation on which there exists a consensus of opinion. It is possible to prove opposite views on just about anything, documented by the views of an impressive array of specialists. Everyone is well equipped and ready to engage in separate monologues.

There is good reason for skepticism when one realizes that some theologians are able to unearth with the greatest of ease every glimmer of fact that might seem to prove the uniqueness of Christianity, while others—and not only antagonists of Christianity—are led by the same sources to opposite results. In our case, it is quite evident that traditional theology has little interest in revealing hellenistic influences on Christianity—which amount to a change of original intentions—or to admit that regardless of interpretative gyrations, Christian origins among the Essenes, the Dead Sea cult, make the novelty of Christianity a matter of mere degree.

Gaitanides, who is Greek, sees all this differently. To him, the Christian concept of salvation is not the beginning but the culmination of a development: "As a matter of fact, hellenistic Greece moved quite consistently toward Jesus; it did so, step by step, in a slowly emerging transition. It actually prepared him and prepared itself for him so that in the end the new faith fell off its tree like a ripened fruit. The vessel had been molded in advance, and it accepted the new content quite readily. Christ did not arrive unexpected. He did not come as a surprise. The spirit that was given birth by him and through him had grown within the womb of the Aegean world of Hellas. Even if it did not conceive it, it did receive it. Yes, I dare say, 'without Aegean Hellenism there would have been no Christianity.'"

If that is so, it should be possible to prove it. I am reminded of the Gospel according to John. The version we know is regarded as the account most heavily influenced by hellenistic tradition. Seen from the time of Jesus' death, it belongs to the last-completed writings of the New Testament. John, who also wrote the Revelation, is supposed to have lived on the Greek island of Patmos in the Aegean Sea, close to the Turkish coast. This fourth Gospel, regarded as the most profound and beautiful, never mentions the word "church," but speaks frequently of love, and is closer to Paul's suffering mystique than the other three Gospels. Even more than suffering, however, John emphasizes enlightenment. In any event, the Gnostic influence, as well as Stoic-Platonic concepts, are in evidence—Greek ideas that have influenced our world.

Looking through Schneider's history of thought in Christian antiquity, I discover correlations that old-fashioned camouflage theology tends to ignore because they are uncomfortable. "The favorite God of the period," Schneider tells us, "although increasingly enmeshed in profundity, spiritualized and stripped of his natural appearance, is Dionysos. His best-known name is 'The Vine.' In John's Gospel, Christ is called 'the true vine.'" That is not just an image or analogy, as in the vineyard parable of the Old Testament, but an exact parallel to the Dionysos myth. John also uses the symbolism of water being turned into wine that Euripides cites as an ancient Dionysian miracle. Like Dionysos, Jesus is described in John's version as "mad" (10:20), and it is surprising that this word was left untouched by later adapters of the Bible.

During the Lord's Supper, John uses this phrase: "He who eats my flesh and drinks my blood. . . ." We find such a theophageous turn of phrase neither in Paul nor Jesus. In the Dionysos myth, however, the titans chew on the flesh of Dionysos; in the Dionysian rites, the Mainades tear raw meat with their teeth as a sacrament of their oneness with God. The difference lies merely in the degree of cultist spiritualization.

Christ is also the true Heracles. In earlier Christian sources, Jesus' mother does not appear during the Crucifixion, but in John's version she appears at the Cross. Jesus speaks to his mother in the manner of Heracles: "Woman, behold your son!" or in some translations, "Do not weep, Mother . . . the divine Father is calling me. . . . I am coming, Father!" In contrast to the Synoptics, John's Christ dies with the same words as Heracles, "It is finished!"

The Synoptics also know nothing of a favorite disciple at the Cross, but the "disciple whom he loved" (19:26) appears in John as the one who took Christ's mother "home to his own house"; this is the Heracles myth in Christian dress. Again, like Heracles, he does not wish to abandon his followers as if

they were orphans: "I will not leave you desolate. . . ."
(14:18) Un Cornutus speaks of the Heraclean religion in
terms reminiscent of John. Heracles, in this instance, is called
Logos: "Logos does not exist to harm or to punish, but to have."
John uses these words: "Because God did not send his Son into
the world in order to judge the world, but so that the World be
saved through him."

Christ is also the true Aesculapius. John describes a place
of healing in the manner of Epidavros, but Jesus is able
to achieve more since he needs no particular place for his
healing miracles. John's version of the raising of Lazarus also
outdoes its Aesculapian parallel. He uses such Aesculapian
phrases as "when you died, you are not dead," although in
Christianized form.

Such variations and hints, which link the Gospel to hellenistic religions, were quickly understood by their original read-
ers. All served the purpose of representing Christ as the true
fulfillment of all religion, and this strengthened the missionary
appeal. For example, one of the best-known Osiris phrases, to
be found in the form of innumerable grave inscriptions, was
"Give fresh water to the soul!" John's Christ is quoted as saying, "If anyone thirst, let him come to me and drink." (7:37)

The dual connections, "water and spirit" and "water and
blood," which we find in John's Gospel, may be related to the
"blood and spirit" concept of the Isis cult. The third chapter
even deals with what was known about Eleusis at Ephesos. An
encounter at night, a rebirth from above, baptism in water, a
womb that serves for the rebirth of the faithful—all these are
Eleusian elements that could hardly be coincidental.

The external form of Jesus' and Paul's messages express
the messages' internal Hellenization. Taken together, the Gospels contain only eleven quotations from the Old Testament,
and these mainly in the account of Christ's sufferings. There
is no remnant of the Greek Septuagint. Of the Synoptic para-

bles, John selected only the one picturing the good shepherd, the one that came closest to the Greek pastoral scene. There is no lack of sea scenes, nightly encounters, pictures of mountains and wells. The most hellenistic is the scene of Jesus weeping at the grave of his friend.

All important persons associated with Jesus have Greek names in the Gospel according to John. The name Nicodemus is as un-Jewish as his manner and speech. The Greek disciples Philip and Andrew overshadow Peter.

Increasing Hellenization corresponds to an adaptation to the Greek patterns of various cults. However, as Carl Schneider notes, the decisive factor was not the circumstance that Christianity encountered religious forms that it could adapt or on which it could lean—even though at first sight this seems the most striking aspect of the development. What truly mattered most was the fact that there existed spiritual attitudes quite closely related to, and amenable to, Christianity.

Then what was so unique and special about Christianity that enabled it to make such decisive progress? Externally it offered little that was new. What we today, largely because of our ignorance, regard as typically Christian was widely represented by various cults. Even the concept of salvation was not new, although it was no longer the Orthodox Jewish road of appeasing God by means of religious practice, but rather by one's own efforts, "with God's help."

It was no longer a question of making peace between Creator and creature, whereby the creature admitted his failings and forced God through sacrifice to forgive and forget. It was no longer a matter of liberation from sin or guilt, but of salvation of man as whole. Paul and the Greek cults saw eye to eye completely in this matter. Not just a single misstep had to be erased, but Original Sin, the very underlying cause of all fault and error, had to be eliminated. Even this method—no matter how little it had to do with Judaism—was almost entirely identical for Paul and the Greeks. Mystical participation in the Divine, "higher than all reason," was the essence. The mystic believer could achieve salvation wherever man realized the divine within himself, whether in abstract belief or ritual action—wherever he knew God because God knew him.

The concept of the "chosen band" of initiates and selected individuals was also common. Just as the mysteries knew various steps of understanding and membership—like the Essenes of Jesus' own origins—so did Paul, possibly by a different route, arrive at the concepts of predestination, divine predetermination, which he describes in the ninth chapter of his letter to the Romans in such horrifying terms: God has chosen some people, while damning others from the start. The potter has it in his hand to create a vessel for positive or negative purposes, whether it means to save or to damn a human being; regardless of how much he tries, he tries; one has either been chosen, or not. (This is one of the cracks in Paul's theology that is difficult, if at all possible, to reconcile with his teaching of salvation of mankind through Christ.)

But no matter how easy it is to add up similar or identical points between Christianity and the hellenistic cult, it remains difficult to re-create the elements separating them so decisively that people would give up their old religion and adopt a new one. We know well enough that Christianity did succeed, but we don't know why. Psychological motives cannot be documented; there are no witnesses who speak on these points. The usual explanation, that the new teaching simply had to succeed because it was "the truth" or "God's word," is only an expression of faith. It does not explain the circumstances. After all, the competing cults were making these very same arguments.

Naturally, we can try to discover the motives for this success because psychological reactions vary far less than do the circumstances that bring them about. There are, for instance, many ways of creating fear. But the image of fear, and man's reaction to rescue from it, have remained the same through the centuries.

Regardless of the wish for salvation, man has forever sought to achieve it by means of specific acts or a specific attitude. The power of mercy was as little known to Jesus as it was to the other cults. As in all other religions, correct action, man's reaction to God's command, was of decisive importance. That is why Jesus answered the question of what was the highest commandment by saying: "You shall love the Lord your God with all your heart and all your soul, and with all your mind. This is the great and first commandment. And a second is like it: You shall love your neighor as yourself. On these two commandments depend all law and the prophets." (Matt. 22:37–40)

Anyone who could not manage that, as had Paul at that time, must have had a guilty conscience; salvation, then, did not come from above but from within man—through personal action, not through God. Man, not God, had to make the adjustment. Man, not God, had to make a sacrifice. That is what Jesus had said.

And then comes Paul and proclaims the exact opposite. Not man, but God, has to make the adjustment, using his "Son" as a sacrifice in order to eradicate Adam's Original Sin. Man only has to believe in this salvation from guilt, sin, and death, and there it is! Every new sin he commits is forgiven in advance as long as he is penitent about it. Now, man is in the clear with God, entirely without a personal sacrifice. He is saved even before he has to do anything about it. Paul himself may not have put it quite so simply, or thought of it in such crude terms. But he can be understood and interpreted in just this way. And many, without a doubt, understood him this way.

Paul's offer, unique in the history of religion, was tempting. One really couldn't achieve forgiveness and salvation more conveniently, and I can well imagine that this was one of the reasons for the rapid acceptance of his new teaching. At first glance, and by comparison with other cults and religions, it provided a much better deal. That the long-promised forgiveness had eventually to be earned through a "Christian life" may not have been obvious to everyone. Otherwise, Paul would not have had to use such acid phrases when he talked about the way of life in Corinth and Galatia. Even with Paul, salvation was not available for free. The difference was simply that he did not make a promise of salvation contingent on an appropriate earlier life, God rather than man had to make the actual sacrifice. Others offered salvation as a dividend; Paul gave it on credit.

This factor, seen psychologically, was the big temptation offered by Paulist teaching, even though Paul was certainly not aware of it. His own life had not provided salvation from law and death as an easy advance on later services, but rather it had had to be earned through his difficult struggle for insight. He did not find ready-made what he passed on as a revealed truth. Mercy and conciliation did not fall into his lap. He had struggled for decades to arrive at a clear conscience and agreement with God. Paul had not believed in credit until he saw the blinding light near Damascus that caused his conversion.

But it remains a fact, nevertheless, that the God who must sacrifice himself to achieve conciliation with his creature is Paul's "invention," which can be explained biographically on the basis of Paul's own search for a merciful God. This reversal is, in terms of religious history, the decisive new element that Paul offered in his missionary pleas for Christianity. By using this reinterpretation of Christ's life and death, Paul met a basic need in man's soul.

9

A FAITH FOR THE POOR

WE ARE used to thinking of the spread of Christianity as a matter of course, almost as if it had been inevitable, an act of nature. A number of elements support and strengthen this impression.

External conditions, in the nearly uniform culture of the Mediterranean, were perfect. According to one Church historian, Walther von Loewenich, writing in *Die Geschichte der Kirche* (*A History of the Church*), "there were no linguistic barriers to surmount, because Paul could communicate everywhere in Greek." The author goes on: "In addition, the New Testament was written in the language commonly used at that time. This linguistic uniformity was a tremendous boon to a religion based on the message of The Word. Further, the Roman Empire had extended uniformity of law and expanded traffic wherever it was in control. The ruins of Roman highways, which linked the body of the Empire like strong arteries, bear witness to heavy traffic. . . . The countries located on the shores of the Mediterranean were closely linked by regularly scheduled boat traffic. Although it does not bear comparison with present-day shipping—it was limited to the summer months and coastal waters—it is remarkable to read that one Phrygian businessman made no less than seventy-two trips to Rome. It is, therefore, not surprising that during this period, and the following centuries, large exchanges of population were taking place. Nearly all the leading theologians of the second and third centuries, although active in the West, had migrated from the East. . . . This exchange of populations naturally offered many opportunities for missionary work."

Internal conditions were apparently equally favorable to the spread of the new teaching. While the old gods were not ridiculed, official deities were encountering a good deal of doubt. At a time when Emperor Augustus had himself hailed as the "Savior of the World," people were ready to look for their Savior elsewhere. "It is a multicolored picture," Von Loewenich writes, "which the era of syncretism, of a melting-together presents during this period of the Empire. Next to detached skeptics, fanatic mystics have their day; the most refined spirituality competes with crude superstition, often both within the same person. Secret and tiny sects exist simultaneously with the grandiose and official State Cult."

People were ready to accept a new and unknown God, and there was no lack of reform movements that sought to halt the slackening of morals that Paul, speaking as a preacher of penitence, presents in his Letter to the Romans as a departure from God: "And since they did not see fit to acknowledge God, God gave them up to a base mind and to improper conduct. They were filled with all manner of wickedness, evil covetousness, malice. Full of envy, murder, strife, deceit, malignity, they are gossips, slanderers, haters of God, insolent, haughty, boastful, inventors of evil, disobedient to parents, foolish, faithless, heartless, ruthless. Though they know God's decree that those who do such things deserve to die, they not only do them, but approve those who practice them." (Romans 1:28–32)

Traveling preachers of antique philosophies mainly advocated in the manner of Stoic instructions stating that true happiness was to be achieved by a sensible, natural lifestyle and the practice of virtue. It was often difficult to separate "pagan" from Christian ethics, particularly in the case of the Stoic Seneca. As Von Loewenich puts it: "Nero's teacher Seneca, who was eventually ordered to open the imperial pupil's veins, appeared to many circles within the old church as so Christian in his instructions that he was suspect of secret adherence to Christianity, and his antagonists even invented an exchange of letters between Paul and Seneca."

It is easy to understand, therefore, that the concept of neighborly love and divine mercy found fertile ground in the Empire. Nevertheless, Paul's offer of salvation was nowhere as easily convincing as has later been alleged. It had, after all, one great disadvantage. It offered salvation by the national deity of a nation that had been dominated by outsiders for hundreds of years, first by the Greeks and later by the Romans; their God had obviously failed, and no Messiah had appeared to restore the people's freedom and religious prestige. The one Messiah, whom the Jews never accepted as their Savior, had been crucified by the Romans as a political criminal. What did this Paul mean when he said that a political criminal, an insignificnt Jew who had been put to death, had been chosen by an "unknown God" to take the world's guilt upon himself and overcome death?

Orthodox Jews knew of no suffering Messiah, and to the Romans, crucifixion was the worst of all fates. Although Paul's teachings about mercy and divine forgiveness were attractive, the type of conciliation he advocated was not. One is tempted to say that Paul might have had more success without invoking Jesus. The life story of Rabbi Jesus was an obstacle to the expansion of Paulist Christianity, which is one reason why the figure of Jesus became increasingly obscured and was finally wrapped in the mantle of divinity until nothing was left of Jesus the human being.

Paul, as yet, knew nothing of this trend toward divinization. To him, Jesus was a normal man, "born of woman." But what could prompt a Greek or Roman to find personal significance in Jesus' fate and Paul's teaching? Was the concept of salvation by itself sufficiently strong to overcome its built-in handicaps and contradictions, or was something else needed? What was it, in this new teaching, that acted to confirm it, to offer new hope to men and women? What prompted people to let themselves be tortured to death by Nero or be thrown to the lions?

"An idea is strong," says Erich Fromm in *Psychoanalysis and Religion*, "only if it is grounded in a person's character structure. No idea is more potent than its emotional matrix. The psychoanalytic approach to religion then aims at the understanding of human reality behind the thought systems. . . . What men think and feel is rooted in the structure of their characters, which, in turn, are at least partly formed by the total pattern of their existence; or, to be more precise, by the socio-economic and political structure of their society."

It is the same with religions. They, too, respond to the pattern of a given period and to a specific mode of life. A religion doesn't just happen; it evolves as several factors combine, begin to have influence on each other, and provide mutual support. It gains identity at the moment when its demands and offers find resonance with a group of people.

Let us start from the premise that Paul's idea of salvation through the Cross applied to all people and had been proclaimed to all. It must therefore be significant that early Christianity was almost entirely made up of people who, in the class structure of the period, stood at the very bottom of the social ladder. Rabbi Jesus' followers were fishermen, despised publicans, outcasts, political extremists. Those who responded to Paul were the propertyless, the exploited and the slaves, and, of course, women. The only difference was that Jesus' followers were mostly country folk, while Paul's came exclusively from the urban proletariat.

All in all, it was those who "labor and are heavy laden" (Matt. 11:28) who turned to the new faith, people to whom Jesus had promised the heavenly kingdom, although a camel might go through a needle's eye before a rich man might enter the Kingdom of God. Everything fits together when we also recall that Jesus was a successor of the Essenes, who advocated poverty, and that the original community of Christians in Jerusalem practiced a primitive form of communism. Jesus himself said that the last should be the first, and that whoever sits at the bottom of the table would be asked by his heavenly host to "move up, my friend." The poor and oppressed would become the masters—all quite enough to consider such a teaching attractive.

Certainly such ideas played a part in the expansion of Paulist Christianity. Paul promised them the equality he himself had to do without: "There is neither Jew nor Greek, there is neither slave nor free, there is neither male nor female" (Gal. 3:28), because with Christ all distinctions were erased. But Paul did not mean this as a call for social renewal. He believed that one should obey authority. So when he spoke of removing the barrier between free men and slaves, he only meant that existing differences had no significance to the faithful. He might just as well have written: Whether Jew or Greek, slave or master, man or woman—it does not matter to God, because he saves the master just as he does the servant.

It would be wrong to assert that Paul promised his followers revolution or an improvement in their status. Instead, he left conditions as he found them, but he dissolved them in a mystical and symbolic manner. Paul does not condemn the rich or play up to the poor. His teaching is not indebted to the Sermon on the Mount or the saying of Jesus. His theme is death; remember: During his time, the Gospels had not yet been written.

Furthermore, Paul did not attribute his proclamation to the reports of eyewitnesses but to divine revelation. He may not even have known the content of the Sermon on the Mount.

What then attracted the poor and the slaves to the new teaching? What did it achieve to give its followers the feeling: "This concerns me personally"? We often read the interpretation that the concepts of love and humanity must have been decisive. But that would seem to correspond more closely to the thought patterns of our own time. To a slave, the very idea that he should love his neighbor—who could only be the master who tormented him—and to love him as himself, would smack of bitter irony.

If new ideas can only flourish where they find a fertile ground in basic emotions, then I would imagine that a totally different identification between the Savior and the saved must have taken place. In contrast to other cults and philosophies, and in contrast to the official cult of God and Emperor, this tentmaker Paul offered the thought that God selected the world's Savior from among the common people. The chosen one had not been one of the prominent, one of the world's masters, but a carpenter's son from Galilee, a simple workingman; God had selected a man from the people.

To the hierarchic order of the time, rigid in its social thinking on all levels, this idea must have been revolutionary. Not master but servant had been chosen; not the victor but the vanquished was to save the world. This was a fate with which the downtrodden, the common man, could identify; it was, after all, his own. When this chosen one suffered "for" others and took their guilt upon himself, those who "labor and are heavy laden" must have understood these words differently from their masters. They were included in this Resurrection for others. He was *their* Savior, one of them. He had given them a new God, who understood them and had chosen one of them. Paul did not create a Gospel for the poor, but for the unrecognized. The fate of the crucified Rabbi Jesus was their own. Their frustrations shared, the outsiders of society saw themselves accepted and appreciated through Jesus. Even if the world failed to acknowledge them, God did.

That, in any case, might be an explanation for the nature of early Christianity as a religion for the poor, even though this psychological explanation does not conform with the concepts of the Church.

But historical developments bolster such a psychological explanation. Today, at least in the industrial countries, Christianity is a religion of the middle class. The workingmen, who had been attracted to Christianity two thousand years ago, are now for the most part estranged from it. At a crucial period in economic history, when the Industrial Revolution was turning men into "slaves" once again, when inhuman conditions prevailed and even children worked twelve to fourteen hours in the factories for starvation wages, Rabbi Jesus had long ago been transformed into the Dearly Beloved Soulmate of the Establishment, governed by the God-given power of a Majesty.

By then, the religion of the poor had been turned into a religion of the prosperous. The very image of Jesus was being drawn in the Nazarene style of the day: a candy-colored, pretty Savior, dressed in a well-ironed robe, who patted innocent children on the head. Society and Savior, the faithful and their divine image tend to look alike. Each period has the Savior it needs, and it also needs the Savior that it has. Motives for belief are as different as times and people; each period seeks its own typical identification. The same Jesus was forced, through two thousand years, to serve emperors and merchants, poor monks as well as the rich.

But I believe that Paulist teaching provided, in addition to the desire for salvation and identification with the Savior, a third opportunity. This may have been its strongest and most lasting contribution to the expansion and continuity of Christianity, because it was unconscious and therefore could not be manipulated. It was the opportunity to revise the relationship of man's God-given environment in relation to God himself.

10

FATHER AND LORD

JESUS called Yahwe his Father. To speak of "Our Father who art in Heaven" is nothing special; nearly everywhere and always, people had called God their Father because it was he who had created everything. A Babylonian hymn speaks of the moon god Sin as "Father, Creator of Gods and Men."

The oldest segments of the Old Testament do not call Yahwe a Father, although he leads his "children" into the Promised Land. One explanation for this curious contradiction lies in the fact that Israel's neighboring religions imagined their gods not as sexless "Creators," but as beings that physically conceived and gave birth like mortal men and women. (To honor these gods and participate in divine creation, man was to practice his sexuality; this point of view is common to all fertility cults.)

As Israel sought to reduce the influence of these other cults, it initially discouraged the Father concept. The Old Testament speaks of Yahwe as the Father much later. That became possible only when the idea of physical creation of a "Son of God" had been replaced by the call of a chosen one. We can trace this development in the words used for the crowning of a king. The formula resembles Near Eastern examples: "Today I have conceived you; you are my son," but it actually means the adoption of an adult as a chosen one; or, more plainly: The formula of adoption means no more than that this king is to execute the will of God, as the son is to act for his father.

Still, even later the Old Testament uses the concept of Father sparingly when it refers to God. There are barely a dozen uses of the word "Father."

The four Gospels, on the other hand, refer to God as the Father about 150 times. This is a quite different world and mentality. God is no longer the strict Lord and Master (this concept is rare in the Gospels), no longer insistent on fear and awe. He has a different function altogether.

In the meantime, God and man have achieved a relationship of trust. This Father is no longer Creator but Protector, and when Rabbi Jesus turns to him, all barriers disappear. He calls him *"Abba,* Father" (Mark 14:36), which conveys an attitude of childlike confidence. In the Aramaic language, *Abba* is baby talk; it is one of the first syllables an infant forms. The same sound pattern of *b* (or *p*) and *a* exists in "Papa." In order to recapture the childlike intimacy shown by Jesus toward his Creator, who is totally lacking in awe-inspiring authority, we should be able to pray, "Our Daddy who is in Heaven, hallowed be thy name. . . ." This has to be understood without any feeling of coyness or blasphemy; it simply means speaking to God as a child does to his father. This form of address is unique. It has no precedent or parallel in Judaism. The awesome "Lord God" had become the Father of those he created; but even this form of address was too indirect for Jesus. It is impossible to speculate on the relative positions occupied by one's father and mother. Honor thy father and mother, for example. But the word *Abba* is without such variations. It implies, quite simply, the most intimate link a man can feel. It is totally personal. It is possible to know many men who are fathers, but only one of them can be called "Daddy."

If we recall that Martin Luther saw God as a harsh and unjustly punishing father, and that Saul the Pharisee suffered from the impossibly severe tasks and commandments imposed by God, Jesus' relation to the divine stands in sharp contrast as a positive, unhampered bond. Jesus saw his contact with God outside a hierarchical pattern.

If we try to transfer Jesus' relation to Yahwe to human contacts, a picture of society emerges that puts greater importance on humane and mutual trust than on authority. It would be a society marked by togetherness rather than by separateness. It would be a world without division into master and servant, and thus in line with Jesus' view of himself. In contrast to Paul, Jesus never spoke of himself as a "servant" of the divine. It would be a world of trust instead of obedience. It would be a world that has never existed.

What did exist was the world of the "servant" (Paul) who served his "Lord" (Christ) because servant and master were characteristic of the society of his time. Jesus never called himself a servant, and he never addressed God as Lord. Paul, on the other hand, speaks of the God on whom he calls so often and about whose conciliation he ruminates incessantly, as Father only four times in his (genuine) Letters. If one reads Paul's letters, the picture of Lord and servant arises constantly: The Lord shows mercy for his servant, whether the Lord is God or Christ. It was through Paul, in particular, that Yahwe's title "Lord" was transferred to Christ. This illustrates the shift in authority that led to the divinization of the Savior.

The emergence of the term "Lord" as a synonym for "God" can be traced to the well-known theological fact that the so-called Septuagint, the Greek translation of the Hebrew Bible, originated the substitution. Depending on one's judgment, this can be seen either as an accidental or a deliberate mistranslation. This translation of the Old Testament, which was made three centuries before Christ, has always been given equal standing with the Hebrew original.

In the Hebrew original, God is referred to as the Lord only nine times. The translations based on the Greek version have, for the most part, repeated the word Lord, or variations of it, dozens upon dozens of times. Thus, the Twenty-third Psalm should not read, "The Lord is my Shepherd," but "Yahwe is my Shepherd." Also, the prayer "May the Lord bless and keep you," originally read, "May Yahwe bless and keep you." Things become more complicated with the popular saying, "The Lord giveth, and the Lord taketh away," because the Hebrew original read, "Yahwe giveth, and the Lord taketh away." And even the Ten Commandments have come down to us with a translation switch: The original is not, "I am the Lord, your God" (Exodus 20:2), but "I am Yahwe, your God."

All this is quite different from what we have known and what we read today. Yahwe was the national God of the Jews, and he was also the God of Rabbi Jesus. God's name was Yahwe, and that is the way we find it today, as thousands of years earlier, in the Hebrew original. Why then this falsification, which has never been corrected? In our day, there can be no excuses for combining "Yahwe" and "Lord" into one single word, even though the spelling in capital letters may vary. If the name is Yahwe, an honest translator has to put it down just that way or he is simply guilty of deliberate fraud. And the word just happens to be Yahwe. Either Christianity acknowledges that it addresses itself to the Jewish God of Jesus, or it reduces its credibility still further, continuing to maintain that what isn't supposed to be, can't be.

While today's mistranslations are inexcusable, the error in the Septuagint can at least be explained, although that doesn't cancel the results. As the holy name of "Yahwe" was not supposed to be pronounced needlessly in Jewish usage—a matter of not taking God's name in vain—the Jews had made a habit of changing the tetragrammaton in the Semitic language, JHWH, by using different vowels to change the sound.

Only centuries after the New Calendar, when there was a danger that Jews in many parts of the world might no longer be able to read a script of consonants even if the correct vowels were added, were certain vocalizing arrangements made; several arrangements of dots and lines were placed under the consonants to assure uniformity. This made it possible to reconstruct the word that the Jews had used as a substitute for the name of God. The method was simple. The consonants JHWH remained, but the vowels of the Hebrew word for "Lord" were placed under it. By this mixture of the consonants for the name of God, JHWH, and the vowels of the word *Adonai,* "Lord," a new word, was formed that had no actual meaning but merely served to block the correct pronunciation of the holy name.

This religious construct, an artificial word born of a taboo, is known to us through the persistent efforts of one sect: it is Jehovah. The translators of the Septuagint had settled for a widely used and elusive variant, the Greek *Kyrios,* or Lord, because it was a title implying masterful control. The "wrong" translation is, therefore, the result of a certain awe before the unmentionable name Yahwe, whose meaning is still not clear. The translation also reflected the conviction that Yahwe is in fact Lord and sovereign Master. *Kyrios* originally meant slaveholder, Lord of the subjugated and legal guardian. The gods of Hellas bear the prefix *Kyrios* in order to convey that might and right are on their side. In a world divided into masters and servants, *Kyrios* clarified the categorical relation of man to God. (In modern Greek, *Kyrios* in used indiscriminately, as we say "Mister," or sometimes, "Sir.")

All this helps to understand Jesus' revolutionary approach to the world around him. By addressing God as a Father, and even a Daddy, who loves but does not control his children, rather than as a superior Lord and ruler, he removed basic social barriers and sociological structures at a time when only the master-servant pattern existed. At the very least, he put it in doubt. Alas, reality remained at first unchanged.

Paul picked up the *Kyrios* title and adjusted his new teaching to the master-servant attitude of his period. He does—and this is interesting—shift everything by one degree: No longer is God known as the Lord (he uses the Greek word *Theos*, thus avoiding the Yahwe concept), but it is "The Risen," Christ the Crucified, who is the Lord, victorious through suffering.

Paul integrated his new teaching into the thought pattern of his time. To be obedient to authority, and to acknowledge the authority of a Lord, reflected the pervading thought and life of the period. The hierarchically organized heavens were reflected on a hierarchically organized earth. There was no freedom in the sense of a freedom to do something, but only as freedom from something, such as freedom from fear. Servant remained servant, although as a Christian he need no longer be afraid. The new teaching does not free him from external circumstances, but helps him to liberate himself internally. Paul, who regarded himself as a servant of Jesus, was able to write: "For you did not receive the spirit of slavery to fall back into fear." He speaks of freedom in a dialectic manner, as something glittering and variable, enabling the human and the divine to act mutually upon each other, to permeate each other.

Next to identification with the Savior, Paul offered identification with existing social order. His theology fits an era that took its internal structure for granted. Paul provided a religious superstructure to a world in which master and servant knew their places.

It is hardly surprising that such a teaching, which helped to stabilize existing conditions, could become a state religion. This may furnish another explanation of why a religion for the poor could so quickly move from servant to master, that a persecuted catacomb religion should evolve into a state religion and replace all other cults and beliefs; it was, after all, a religion that justified existing social systems built on the difference between Lord and follower.

As a result, Occidental Christianity entered a crisis period as soon as this social structure began to crumble and the idea of liberty, equality, and fraternity gained ground. When this happened, millennia of identity within a given style of life and faith broke apart, and the German Catholic handbook *Praktisches Bibellexikon* (*Practical Bible Dictionary*) could say: "As the changing structures of sociology and history have made the concept of 'Lordship' subject to new interpretations and questions, the word 'Lord' can no longer be used in the same way as during a period of unquestioning submission to an absolute master. This transition is bound to affect the understanding and usage of the Christological form of address, if confession to the Lord Jesus Christ is not to seem antiquated."

And yet, the churches act as if nothing had happened. They go right on using the same old categories, as if we were still living in a society of masters and slaves. Paul's world no longer exists. His theology is out of step with contemporary views and feelings. What was once Paul's decisive act, his ability to dramatize his own feelings of guilt and need for salvation so his followers could identify with them, has long since become a dangerous obstacle to an understanding of Jesus' yearning faith. Certainly Paul managed to achieve a breakthrough for his new teachings with the proper means at the right time. He combined his own ideas with an odd mixture of contemporary mysticism, rationalist legalism, and primitive beliefs in sacrifice, welding Greek philosophy and timeless truths to a limited social structure. But for all he achieved, he had to pay the price that, with the decline of these structures, his theology would lose ground.

Of course Paul thought as little about the future as had

Rabbi Jesus. Neither of them expected their eras to last very long. Both expected an early Judgment, and neither had the idea of actually founding a new religion, as did Mohammed later on. They only wanted to tell their contemporaries of God and urge them to repent in time for the Kingdom of God. They taught totally different things. One taught faith in God as a Father; the other taught belief in Jesus as the Lord. Neither could defend himself against the things that were later done to their teachings.

Neither Paul nor Jesus had thought of founding a Church. But, without meaning to, they prepared the ground for it. And just as the death of Jesus marked the beginning of something new—the expansion and change of his teachings—so did the death of Paul open a new chapter: strength and rigidity.

11

EMPEROR AND BISHOP

THE NEW Christian sect was only a little over thirty years old in the year 65 when Paul was executed in Rome under Emperor Nero. Since the year 48, the movement had been split into Jewish and pagan Christians, dating back to the Apostolic Council. In 70, shortly after Paul's death, Jerusalem was destroyed and the Jewish nation dissolved. It looked as if everything had come to an end.

Apocalyptic Judgment had arrived as expected, but the results were very different from the dreams. Now the very Temple, God's Sanctuary, had been destroyed—and no Messiah, no Jesus had appeared to rescue his people. The only thing that remained was trust in the future, a virtually vain hope that held together a few thousand "Christians" among the fifty million people then governed by the *Imperium Romanum*.

Historic realism would have had to assume that these outsiders would succumb and disappear, together with all the other sects and movements of the day. The leader of the pagan Christians had died as ignominiously as had Rabbi Jesus, head of the Jewish Christians. The "Pillars of Jerusalem," Jesus' little band of followers in Jerusalem, had either fled or, like Peter, suffered a martyr's death. (Facts are elusive; Peter's death was prophesied in the Gospel according to John, Chapter 21, verse 19, but not reported; his death in Rome is legend, as is his burial at St. Peter's Basilica in the Vatican.)

In the second half of the first century, the Christian sect found itself scattered around the rim of the Mediterranean from Rome to Jerusalem, from Crete to Macedonia, totally without leadership. It was held together by an oral tradition and the Letters written by Paul. The movement was in constant danger from the very heretics and "false prophets" against whom Paul had warned his followers.

In the midst of this hopeless situation, something remarkable took place. At the very moment that the enthusiasm of a new beginning turned into fear and martyrdom—Nero used the flaming bodies of Christians as torches in his gardens—the scattered movement evolved into a hierarchically organized Church. The authority of the Apostle is replaced by the authority of an organization; into the footsteps of a divinely chosen leader steps the impersonal official. The breath of the Holy Spirit is administered in terms of rank and position.

The first generation of Christians had been able to do without an official text, a book that recorded the history and ideas of the movement. What each member of the first generation had known from his own experience, now had to be defined. What had once been accepted as common knowledge, with mutual help, study, and refinement, now had to be divided into layers of responsibility. Professing Christianity had become a profession.

All this did not happen immediately, and not all at once. Still, it took place with the compulsive drive of a movement that grows beyond the enthusiasms of its first phase, seeks solid patterns, only to freeze into them, inevitably although involuntarily. In this respect, the history of early Christianity is unexceptional. Every religion and ideology has walked down the path from intuition to institution.

And yet, this is a decisive phase. At this seam, this fault, an immortal idea becomes mortal. Whatever we have retained of Rabbi Jesus and his life—despite all distortions and obscurities—has the echo of the absolute; it can neither be repeated nor imitated. It made demands on mankind which, in their timelessness, had an impact far beyond the limited horizons of Galilee.

Paul began to chip away at this truth, reducing it to the egoism of personal salvation that is not achieved by man but by God. Jesus still taught *trust in God*—and the word "trust" is only a translation of the Greek word for "faith"—while Paul taught *belief in Jesus*. The Jesus of the first Gospels knew nothing of an intermediary, someone who places himself between man and God and thereby separates them. But Paul and John of the Gospel reached God only through the intercession of another.

The Church went one step further when it made itself the intermediary between God and man. This shocking concept does not come down to us from the Middle Ages but from the early period of the Church: "No one can have God as a Father, who does not have the Church as Mother." This was written by Cyprian, Bishop of Carthage—a predecessor of Augustine—who coined the famous phrase that "there can be no salvation outside the Church." To this day this formula is the secret Magna Charta and self-justification of all the Churches, although it runs counter to the intentions of Rabbi Jesus, who did not know a church, did not want a church, and did not establish a church, and who found it was quite acceptable if one addressed God in the privacy of one's own little room or in the company of like-minded people.

Jesus wanted the Kingdom of God; Paul wanted salvation from his guilt; the Church wanted itself. Christ failed; Paul was executed; the Church triumphed.

In our time, the Church is widely regarded as untrustworthy, rigid, and encrusted. It turns in a void, like a prayer drum, and what keeps it moving in front of empty pews is not the Holy Spirit but social momentum. The thoughts of Jesus, however, although remote from the Church, remain true to this day. And it was this that helped the new sect to victory in Roman times. Paul's assimilation to Greco-Roman thinking was useful opportunism, but it also planted the seed of eventual destruction. The power of the Church crumbled as soon as a society that thought exclusively in terms of master and servant, superior and inferior, faded. The end came with the disappearance of authority that regarded its position as God-given and was closely linked to the Church. What remained in many places was a Christianity for retirement, an anachronism that has no link to its beginnings. What could have gone wrong all along the line that a young man in his thirties could shake the world, yet now interests mainly those who spend their declining years in the Church?

I am in search of this fault. I want to know when it first appeared. Precisely where is this seam where intuition became institution? Where did eternal truth shrink to human proportions and become mortal?

Perhaps it was at the point where hope was stronger than reality. Perhaps it was the defiance of disappointed hope, since the remarkable transition started just after the deaths of the apostles Paul and Peter and the catastrophe of the year 70. In the midst of this desperate situation, when all accepted leaders had disappeared, the unknown and nameless picked up the remnants and carried on. Just then, when it seemed much too late, some began to write down the life of Jesus while others collected Paul's Letters. They created a substitute authority. Paul's occasional Letters, together with the Gospels, slowly evolved into the psychological beginning of a divinely inspired "Holy Writ."

The authors of the New Testament obviously did not have

the immediate intention of creating a "Holy Writ" because they quite casually began to manipulate historical truth as it fitted their needs and the requirements of the moment.

Contradictions increase with the addition of Gospels and Letters. In their original versions, the Gospels, just like the original community, knew nothing of sacrificial death and justification. Paul, on the other hand, knew the life of Jesus only by hearsay. As a result, within half a century following Paul's death, twelve different and contradictory traditions collided with one another, influenced each other, or remained unreconciled side by side.

The oldest of the four reports on the life of Rabbi Jesus, the Gospel according to Mark, provides the picture of a preacher of penitence who considers himself Israel's Savior but who seeks to disguise this aim. When he fails before the Kingdom of God has arrived, he dies with the cry of desperation, "My God, my God, why hast thou forsaken me?" and this Gospel naturally reflects in its ending the fear and hopelessness of the disappointed disciples.

But Mark's Gospel also contains the three proclamations of suffering (Chapters 8, 9, and 10) in which Jesus allegedly accurately prophesies his own death on the Cross and his Resurrection. Something is wrong here. Either Jesus and his disciples viewed his anticipated *death* as essential Salvation—and if so, their desperation is difficult to understand—or they saw his essential task in his *life*—and then the prophecies about a positive meaning of his death are incomprehensible.

The contradiction is explained if one realizes that the Gospel according to Mark was written about the year 70—perhaps even earlier, while Paul was still alive, although independent of his own interpretation of the death on the Cross—in Asia Minor or elsewhere in the Near East—and afterward reached the communities which through Paul had learned to interpret Jesus' death in different terms. But as they did not wish to change the text itself, they simply inserted the prophetic sections at three points, thus presenting Paul's version of the death retroactively as Jesus' own prophetic words. (The final section of Mark's Gospel, beginning with verse 9, is also not genuine.) This brought the Gospel up to date and, although imperfectly, in line with other material.

Such "prophecies on the basis of events that have already taken place" are called by theologians *vaticinium ex eventu*, a dignified choice of words. They appear in the Bible fairly frequently.

The new sect arrived at its hierarchical structure in a manner resembling these prophecies. Neither Paul nor Jesus, both of whom counted on an early end of the world, had left any sort of instructions for the future. In fact, Jesus had explicitly rejected any sort of rank structure. Once, when the disciples argued as to "which of them was to be regarded as the greatest," he told them: "The King of the Gentiles exercises lordship over them; and those in authority over them are called benefactors. But not so with you; rather let the greatest among you become as the youngest, and the leader as one who serves." (Luke 22: 24–26)

The word "Church," therefore, appears in the four Gospels only twice, and in both cases it might just as well have been translated as "community." That is, in fact, the way Luther translated it, while other versions translate the Greek *ecclesia* as Church in at least one instance. The King James Version as well as the Revised Standard Version follow this pattern; in Matthew 16:18 we read, according to the RSV, "And I tell you, you are Peter, and on this rock I will build my church, and the powers of death shall not prevail against it." It is from this quotation that the Roman Catholic Church derives the concept of the Papacy.

As Jesus did not really intend to found a Church because he expected the King of Heaven, this quotation, if it is authentic, must have had a different meaning from today's concept of the Church. True, the Greek word *ecclesia* means "church" in the modern sense, but the original meaning of it was a different one.

I find an explanation in the Jerusalem Bible, which contains this comment on the sentence in Matthew: "The Hebr. *qahat* which the Greek renders *ekklesia* means 'an assembly called together'; it is used frequently in the O.T. to indicate the community of the Chosen People, especially the community of the desert period, cf. Ac 7:38 [the RSV uses 'congregation' in this instance]. Certain Jewish groups, among them the Essenes of Qumran, regarded themselves as the chosen remnant of Israel (Is 4:3+) which was to survive in 'the latter days.'"

Here, too, Jesus provided no instructions for the future but withdrew to the Qumran cloister, the goal of his philosophical and spiritual background. He specifically linked Peter, or Bar-Jona ("He who lives outside"), with the Qumran community in the desert; he thereby associated his disciples indirectly with the Essenes, but he did not establish a new church. Most certainly Jesus did not name a successor. Even according to Matthew, he dies with the outcry of desperation at a God who had forsaken him. His messianic task had failed. There was nothing beyond the Cross.

Neither a church as such nor any equivalent organization can be derived from the Gospels. But neither did Paul, whose missionary zeal was based on his expectation of an early heavenly kingdom, have the establishment of a church in mind. While he did found communities or congregations that were linked with each other, they did not at first have an official hierarchy. On the contrary, being "free of the law," they were to rest on the spirituality of mutual love. The ecstatic communities of that time knew neither priest nor office, but practiced a "common priesthood." There was no differentiation between priest and layman. In principle, everyone could baptize, experience revelations, or act as a prophet because Paul insisted on a basic difference between religion and law: "Christ has saved us from the curse of the law."

And yet it was Paul who, through his master-servant ideas, actually established the first order of rank: "And God has appointed in the church first apostles, second prophets, third teachers, then workers of miracles, then healers, helpers, administrators, speakers in various kinds of tongues." (Cor. 12: 28)

Some regard the legalized organization of the Church as the most tragic development in Christianity. Nevertheless, if they were to avoid chaos, the communities had to have some sort of order. Schneider notes: "Hesitantly at first, and still competing with the freedoms of ecstasy in love in Greece, the Church became a legally constituted body based on a *jure divino* (divine law). This process was helped by the legal traditions of the East, Rome and the Old Testament. The community of love became an ecclesiastical discipline, a common priesthood grew into a legally unassailable hierarchy of office, and those speaking with the Spirit became legally protected Bishops; ecstatics were replaced by advocates, and finally God's relationship to man was governed by a legal code. The New Testament is the first evidence of this clash. The Paulist Church of the Spirit, which had assembled inspired Christian enthusiasts to celebrate the Lord's Supper and to works of charity, was replaced by an organized cult which at first had an aristocracy of office and then a monarchic organization."

One is forced to think back to the original community in Jerusalem and its "Pillars," to the messianic-oriented counter-régime to the Sanhedrin, which had its Apostles and deacons. One recalls that the Jerusalem community had the right to summon Paul and examine his teaching. These were not yet legal positions, but offices based on personal authority. Nowhere in the Old Testament is there a reference to a monarchic bishopry. Only in the so-called "Pastoral Letters" of the New Testament is there a reference to firm organization. Suddenly, Christians are told, "Learn to obey." These Letters (the First and Second Letters of Paul to Timothy, his Second Letter to the Thessalonians, and the Second Letter of Peter) were written between the years 70 and 125, after the deaths of both Paul and Peter, although they are attributed to them.

A new authoritarian sound is heard. "Be subject for the Lord's sake to every human institution" (Peter 2:13) and "Servants, be submissive to your masters in all respect" (Peter 2:18), or "Clothe yourselves, all of you, with humility toward one another." In Timothy there is a reference to the office of bishop (I Tim. 3:1), and we read: "Let all who are under the yoke of slavery regard their masters as worthy of all honor." (I Tim. 6:1)

Right along we are told that these writings were made by either Paul or Peter. And yet these Letters are so much forgeries as the prophecies recorded after the event. Theological research is, in this respect, remarkably in agreement: These Letters were composed after the death of both Apostles. But their aim is obvious. They served as substitute authority, through the fraudulent use of the names of Paul and Peter, in order to justify a hierarchy of office for which there was no basis in the New Testament. The nameless authorities who had taken over where the Apostles had left off were like relay runners who suddenly moved in a totally different direction from those envisaged by Jesus and Paul. To achieve order, they were willing to restrict freedom.

The chain can be identified by its individual links. Jesus still spoke to God as a trusting child, calling him *Abba* or "Daddy." Paul refers to Christ as "Lord," and Paul's successors lengthen the chain by an additional link: to the Lord God and the Lord Jesus Christ, they add the Lord Bishop. Ignatius of Smyrna said, "Without the Bishop, you can do nothing" because the Christian is to obey his bishop just as Christ obeyed God, so that "Whoever obeys his Bishop is honored by God, but whoever acts without his Bishop serves the devil." Or as Ignatius puts it another way, "Whoever belongs to God and Jesus Christ, stands with his Bishop."

At one time anyone whose life qualified him could be elected bishop, but this was soon ruled as improper. After that, only someone who had followed a hierarchial career could aspire to be a bishop. Two hundred years after Paul's death, the ecclesiastical bureaucracy had achieved perfection, and the bishop's post was the culmination of advancement within the system. Only the bishop was authorized to undertake a baptism. Only he was therefore qualified to decide who might achieve eternal bliss, and who would be passed by; the rest had to remain common church folk, the unqualified masses.

There was no pretense at equality. Division between clergy and laity, something unknown to Jesus, was established. Soon it was maintained that anyone who accused or criticized "Peter" was guilty of accusing God. Cyprian was the first to demand that one should stand up before a bishop, much like the custom before a pagan idol. One shameful result of this trend was that bishops, who previously were addressed as "Brother," demanded, 150 years after the birth of Christ, to be addressed as "Lord," as if they were God himself. As Carl Schneider put it, "The divine legitimacy of the Ruler had returned, just as in any Cult of the Ruler; it was in no way Christian."

Where is the fault, the seam in the fabric of the development of the Church? It is worth sepeculating what Jesus would have done if he had been forced to establish a church. To this day, a Jewish clergyman, a rabbi, has essentially no function beyond the knowledge that might lift him above other believers. Neither then nor now does the Jewish faith know a division between clergy and laity. No rabbi may hold a religious service unless an additional nine men are present. Alone, he is nothing. He is no intermediary, no link between man and God, and the Chief Rabbi of Israel, the "High Priest," is no nearer to God than the plain Jew who prays at the Wailing Wall.

If Rabbi Jesus had ever decided to establish his own religion, it would not have been Christianity as we know it.

Perhaps the origin of our Church is to be found in the Greek mystery cults. The cult of Dionysos had at the head of its communities a "hero," who may have occupied something of the position of an intermediary between God and the community; but we do not know that this was the case. Homer, at any rate, spoke of "bishops" eight hundred years before Christ; they were gods who acted as Episcopoi, as protectors and guardians of the world and man. Throughout, the word has had a religious sound.

Later on, the Episcopoi were the favorite characterization of the philosophy of the Cynics. They used it to describe the deputies of the deity on earth, those who supervised everything. We seem to be getting closer. But the Greek cult of the gods never had a very authoritarian pattern. Fate, or *moira*, stood higher than the gods themselves. A Christian bishop was more exalted than that; he could decide on his own whom to free and whom to bind.

The seam between the God of Jesus and the God of Christianity runs somewhere else. We can see exactly where the Roman citizen Paul reversed the revolutionary teaching of Rabbi Jesus where it fitted the master-servant pattern of the Roman Empire, whose ruler had himself feted as a savior and who was preceded in public processions by imposing standards just as the bishops did later on.

Certainly, Paul did not create the Church. But if he had, it would look the way it eventually turned out to be. Because, as Schneider puts it, it was the Church's tendency to build its administration and leadership "not in the democratic way of most hellenistic cults, nor on the equality of Judaism and other eastern religions, but along the monarchic-dictatorial lines of the hellenistic state cults and the Roman Emperor cult."

The commandment to love became one of obedience; equality of the Children of God became subordination to the bishop-stepfather. The charitable conciliation of man and God, child and Dad, turned into a broker's monopoly of mercy at the hands of men.

12

HERESY VICTORIOUS

No ONE can tell for sure just when the Church, as such, was formally established. It probably was never specifically organized at all. Rather, it evolved over the centuries until it became what it is today.

A similar development took place in ecclesiastical dogma. Just as the Church Establishment achieved its form slowly in its exchange with the world around it, so was its teaching the result of an exchange of ideas.

And just as in the case of the Establishment itself, this road led away from everything that had been originally conceived. The historical Jesus, feted at his entry into Jerusalem as the nation's spiritual and political Savior, knew nothing of sacrificial death and Resurrection. He never thought of himself as the embodied Son of God, but rather as the "son of man." He did not dissolve the law but sought to strengthen it by adding to physical sin, the sin of thought. Thus, for example, in the sixth commandment, just looking at a woman and desiring her amounts to adultery. The historical Rabbi Jesus was a strongly law-abiding Jew.

The theologian Adolf von Harnack writes in *Das Wesen des Christentums* (*The Nature of Christianity*): "Jesus permitted no doubt that God may be found in the law and the prophets, and has indeed been encountered there." Von Harnack reminds us that that Jesus' popular parables "are innocent of any 'Christology'" but illustrate the major points Jesus wanted to make exactly: "Whoever twists and overinterprets simply injures the simplicity and greatness of Jesus' preachings in their most important aspects."

And it is, of course, quite true that Jesus—as we can see from the Gospels—conciliates man with God without any sort of reference to the Cross, without any kind of "Christology." He says, "Your faith has helped you." And that was enough: this very faith that God could make the blind see, if he wanted to, and make the lame walk, as long as men have trust and obey the laws. We have simply forgotten to keep this clearly in mind because the churches are constantly interpreting the Gospels in the Paulist sense. They falsify them, as if one could put Jesus' teachings on the same level as the "Christology" that Paul invented later on, but that basically has nothing to do with it.

"It is a desperate assumption," Von Harnack writes, "to maintain the Jesus preachings were only something preliminary, that everything contained in them had to be seen in a different light after his death and Resurrection; indeed, that some of it had to be put aside as inappropriate. No, these proclamations were plainer than the churches wish to admit. . . . Jesus moved man closer to the great questions, promised God's mercy and charity and demanded this decision: God or Mammon, eternal or mortal life, soul or body, humility or self-righteousness, love or selfishness, truth or lie. Within this circle lie all relevant matters."

But the Church would not leave well enough alone. Ever since Paul, it insisted on pushing the Son of Man farther and farther away, substituting the Son of God piece by piece, until he became a God himself. It was not Jesus who placed the sentence, "I am the Son of God" in the Gospel, and whoever puts it there as equivalent to others actually patches something into the Gospels. Von Harnack notes, "Not the Son but the Father alone belongs in the Gospel, exactly as Jesus had proclaimed."

There is a vast difference between what is today presented as Christianity and the original teachings of Jesus. If one is so inclined, this development can be traced into every theological crevice. Schneider says that "it is rarely possible in the history of religion to observe the development of myth and history into a teaching as clearly as in the history of Christology. To begin with, our source material is quite extensive, and many forms of teaching are without gaps. And we also know the forces engaged in formulating these changes."

To do this sort of historical detective work properly, we would have to deal in detail with the Greek schools of philosophy and the various mystery cults of the Near East and Greece, as well as with Gnosis, an early target of New Testament defenders. We would also have to study a whole series of fascinating disputes with heresies of which the "Fathers of the Church," the spiritual leaders of the day, have spoken at length. It would be possible in every case to show that the young Church attracted alien ideas, whether to absorb them, change them, or reject them.

The pressure was enormous. The Christian sect had barely been established. It was still without a firm teaching and found itself controversial, embattled, and persecuted by Emperor Domitian in the year 95. Furthermore, it had to devote its decisive years of early growth to a variety of intricate questions.

Even if I tried to follow all these lines of inquiry, the emerging picture could only, by its very vastness, become unclear. I therefore shall only draw the outlines, noting the points of historical development that some regard as victories for Christianity, although others see them as the most tragic misfortunes that could possibly have befallen it on the road of its development.

Five major stations dramatized the pro and con of the young Church and placed their mark on it, five teachings that proved a challenge to the Church. Of these, only one was accepted as correct; another one was rejected; and three were condemned. Tragically, the Church did not condemn the false teachings but suppressed those that pointed toward original concepts.

The first and decisive deviation from an original concept is Paul himself, who turned Jesus against his will into an intermediary and a "Lord" who places himself between God and man. The first three Gospels had indicated how, *through* Jesus, man could arrive at faith and trust in God; Paul taught that one had to believe *in* Jesus in order to reach God. There is no need to repeat this here. But we must make one observation: Although, compared to the teaching of Jesus, this concept is like a heresy, a false teaching, a deviation from an original concept, the Church never categorized it as such.

The second deviation, one that the Church rejected but that it has never overcome, has no specific author. It is Gnosticism, a word that covers a collection of many and varied salvation movements of late antiquity. Its origin is unknown, but it is assumed that it developed in the eastern Mediterranean area of Syria and Palestine. One of its main centers was Egypt's Alexandria, and its most important spokesmen lived between A.D. 120 and 200.

All Gnostic movements share a search for insight, knowledge, understanding—all three words represented by the Greek *gnosis* —which might lead to the world's escaping its darkness and returning to an existence of illumination. That meant man needs to gain knowledge of his own origin and destination in order to save himself. In answer to this ultimate question of every religion, Gnosticism developed a series of partly, quite fantastic cosmological systems designed to link man and the universe. The actual world in this case is the area of light in the upper spheres, while man is trapped in the darkness of ignorance and the body. Whoever achieves the necessary Wisdom, or *Sophia*, can gain access to the area of light and be saved.

This does not sound "un-Christian" at all. The vocabulary of Paul and John was clearly influenced by Gnosticism, as were the Essenes. This respected, and for a long period largest, church within Christianity was not devoted to any saint or Apostle, but to "Holy Wisdom," to *Hagia Sophia*. The men who first engaged in an interpretation of Scripture were probably Gnostics. The oldest commentary in existence, an interpretation of the Gospel according to John, comes from the pen of a Gnostic.

Still, the Church battled the Gnostics. This battle is incomprehensible. Where was the danger to Christianity, considering that the thoughts of the period were permeated by Gnostic ideas and that the New Testament had been shaped by the impact of the Essenes as well as by Greek Gnosis?

We can only guess. Perhaps we should remember the fears of a new sect that it might be regarded as offering "nothing special," possibly an anxiety about the similarity between the two sets of ideas. Church historian Heinrich Kraft writes in *Die Kirchenväter* (*The Church Fathers*, 1966): "There were pagan cult groups which included Christ among their Gods; there were Christians who regarded a syncretic interpretation of their faith as acceptable; there were philosophers who believed that they had found Platonic insights in Christian revelation; as well as any conceivable number of other combination and mixtures. But one thing was not possible: to find anything in this mixture that was contrary to the nature of Christianity."

As Christianity had itself partly evolved from Gnosticism, there now existed the danger of a leveling-out. Gnosis was in the process of reabsorbing Christianity. Naturally, the new sect defended itself and suddenly fought the very thing that had once contributed to its diffusion.

But the most decisive factor was probably, as Kraft points out, that the Gnostics had no regard for the "historical uniqueness of Christ," and this is probably the fundamental reason for Christianity's rejection of Gnosticism. After all, if the Christ whom Paul proclaimed and had seen in visions was not unique, then this particular road to salvation was also not essential, implying that the transformation of Jesus into a "Lord" who towers over all others was also wrong.

The struggle against Gnosticism was most certainly centered on the increasing divinization of Christ; Gnostics did not need such an elevated intermediary. The Gnostic position, "It is the revealed and proper aim of those who possess Gnosis to become God," contains a personal solution and did not confirm the religious master-servant theme.

While the Church rejected Gnosis, it did not overcome its influence in one decisive area: The contrast between body and soul, closely identified with Christianity, had its un-Christian beginning with Gnosticism.

The sharp division of an upper world of light from a lower world of darkness assumed that the world was no longer held together by one Creator but by two warring principles. The Dualism of Gnostic thought assumes that good and evil are at war with each other, that man is in the clutches of evil and has to do everything possible to free and save himself. According to Herder's biblical encyclopedia: "The Gnostic theory of the world evolution explains this unhappy situation with the tragic fall of a light figure, or the struggle between light and darkness. Only Gnosis, offering safety from this virtually physical disaster and enlightenment concerning the Self and its lost existence, reminds man of his nature and origin and shows the way to a return, or ascension, into his native 'home.'"

This is the same pessimistic Dualism known from the ancient levels of the Bible. The Old Testament, too, knows of the fall of a figure of light: Lucifer, the fallen angel, who later within the Church became the evil principle of the Devil and who is known to Jesus. "I saw Satan fall like lightning from heaven." (Luke 10:17) The Old Testament even reports a bet between God and Devil, the principles of good and evil. The guinea pig was Job, whom God turns over to the Evil One for an experiment in Temptation. And finally, Gnosticism desired no more than God's first creatures when they were tempted by the snake—symbol of evil: to know good and evil in order "to be like God."

But, though Jesus knows this split world, talks to the evil spirits of the possessed, and permits them to enter a herd of swine, and although his disciples say, "Lord, even the demons are subject to us in your name!," his separation of good and evil forces has nothing to do with the Dualism of two equally strong principles. For him, there exists only one Creator of Heaven and Earth, and everything, even his antagonists, have been subject to that Creator from the start.

Jesus did not advocate a flight from the body. Instead, he healed in order to make ailing bodies well. He would not have compared bread and wine with body and blood if he had regarded the human body as something sinful that needed to be overcome. According to Jewish faith, the body was God's creation and therefore not a bad thing at all. From this idea developed the concept of a physical Resurrection, whose proponents were not the least bit eager to use this favorable opportunity to rid the soul of its alleged prison.

Gnostic Dualism of body and soul, of the good and the evil principles, led to the idea of asceticism, a conscious effort to eliminate the body, which is a mere prison of the soul.

This philosophy entered Christianity by way of religious Gnosticism. Jesus knew nothing about it. Otherwise, he would not have been accused of associating with gluttons and drunks while the disciples of John the Baptist were fasting.

Whatever it was that young Christianity rejected in Gnosticism, it accepted disdain for the body. We know it not only from the mortification of the body by the pious of the Middle Ages, but also from rejection of the world, which drove the first monks into the desert. It persists among Christians to this day, always ready to pounce when someone enjoys life. Christianity accepted this pessimistic, downbeat view of Creation because it later turned out to be quite practical. It had the advantage of eliminating the need to look after the well-being of the serf and the oppressed, of seeking to bring about basic changes. The Church distributed soup among beggars, while telling them that life in Paradise would be happier as well as bodyless. It reassured "all who labor and are heavy laden" but did not give them any basic help because their essential "home" was not of this world, but in a luminous Other World. This was the pessimism of late antiquity, which ignored the implication of Jesus' word that the Kingdom of God would not only, or first, appear in Heaven but "also on this earth."

13

THE REVOLUTION THAT FAILED

THE THIRD deviation from Christianity was that of a man whom St. Polycarp of Smyrna called a "first-born of Satan" and who was described by others as "a filthy pig" and a "repulsive blasphemer." His name was Marcion. The son of a bishop, he was born at the close of the first century in Sinope. We don't know the reason, but he was expelled from his home community, a Greek town on the Black Sea, and made his way by a circuitous route to Rome. There, he made the local Christian community a large gift of money, but they expelled him, too, and—we are assured in the historical literature—gave him back the money.

In the year 144, Marcion decided to found a church of his own, and his success was tremendous. As early as 150 Justin reported that Marcion's teachings had gathered followers everywhere. Many believed that he was "the sole possessor of truth." Tertullian wrote a total of five books against him, saying that his heresy had covered the world.

Marcion's "false doctrine" was a very simple line of thought, apparently based on the pessimism and Dualism of the Gnostics, which led him to a new and unusual theology. Walter von Loewenich summarizes it as follows: "We hear from Marcion's ecclesiastical antagonists that Marcion thought poorly of the Creation. He argues that if the world was really created by one God, then this God must be inferior. When Marcion reads in the Old Testament about Creation, he feels that this Old Testament God fits the world perfectly. . . . According to Yahwe, the Old Testament God, the principle of an eye for an eye, a tooth for a tooth, is operative. He is the God of the strongest vengeance, of unbendable justice, of demanding law. But Jesus canceled the law and proclaimed mercy, forgiveness, and love. This gives Marcion the pattern of a confrontation between two Testaments and two Gods. They confront each other in an effort of conciliation: the just God of the Old Testament who created this bad world, and the good, unknown and strange God, who cannot be recognized from the time of Creation, whom Christ proclaimed."

Marcion had much the same experience as Paul. Marcion was unable to recognize the Father in Yahwe, the one who cares lovingly for his children. But he solves the problem in a manner different from Paul. Whereas Paul found the explanation that the very same strict God of the Old Testament made an offer of mercy through his "Son," thus becoming a God of Love, Marcion winds up with two Gods: the avenging Creator-God of the Old Testament, and the God of love of the New Testament—a separation that has remained alive to this day, although Jesus did not know it and although the Church condemned Marcion.

The idea of two Gods had dual results.

According to Marcion, Jesus had proclaimed a totally new God. Thus, all the Gospels and Letters that still referred to the Old Testament God must be forgeries. Marcion was, therefore, the first to put together a "Canon," a guideline to the New Testament, that contained only the "purified" versions of Luke's Gospel and ten of Paul's Letters. He rejected all other writings as well as the Old Testament. Marcion was the first, in other words, who sought to demolish Christianity's bridge to the Old Testament. But he did not do it for "anti-Semitic" reasons, as others did later when they tried hard to turn Rabbi Jesus into an "Aryan," in order to deny his Jewish origins.

Marcion's establishment of a God of vengeance and of a God of love led to a second and surprising concept. He maintained that Jesus had not been a real human being at all, but a God who had disguised himself as a man. Von Loewenich writes: "This is the miracle of Jesus' appearance: the good God is touched by the fate of mankind that he did not create. He therefore sends his son, who certainly cannot become a creature of the bad God and must therefore clothe himself in a pseudo-body while on earth. He preaches his Gospel, which in the world of the Creator-God must call for a total reversal of values. He pays his ransom to the Creator-God with death on the cross. By doing this, he wins us for the good God. Thus, Christ is saved, but his body still belongs to the Creator-God. He must therefore break the power of the body with all his might; his weapon is the most severe form of asceticism and, above all, sexual deprivation."

The Church rejected the idea of two Gods. It acknowledges the "Creator of Heaven and Earth," who is also the "Father" of Christ.

But here again, the Church rejected one thing while retaining another. It continued to argue about the cliché of an Old Testament God of vengeance (which isn't true) and of the God of love, who eventually became the rather saccharine "Good Lord." Above all, it has been much concerned about the idea of a pseudobody and asceticism. After all, the heretical idea that Jesus had not been a real person corresponded exactly to the trend of the period, which eventually elevated the historic Rabbi Jesus into divinity. Certainly this concept, known as Docetism, went too far when it sought to deny Jesus' humanity altogether; but the Church itself later hit on the dialectical wording that Christ had been "simultaneously a true man and a true God." Still, Docetism contributed to the increasing rigidity of several thoughts, which later became dogma, which could be more easily explained with Christ's pseudohumanity.

For instance, the problem of Virgin Birth, without masculine participation, could be explained with the observation that Christ had, after all, not been a real person, so that it was sufficient if Mary was merely "overshadowed" by God. Whatever that may mean, it adds up to Christ's body having been unreal.

Docetism also helped to prove quite easily that Jesus was free of sin because only a mortal body can sin, not the God who is inside it.

And finally, Docetism eliminated the difficulties created by Christ's death. Christ, who, according to the Gospel of John, had been created from the beginning of the world, was himself never subjected to death or Resurrection. What died had been his pseudobody. If something visibly went up to Heaven, the "it" was merely the pseudobody. The God of love did not permit his Son to die on the Cross; he only pretended that he did.

Marcion's teachings, by their very simplicity, are somehow naïvely attractive. One must give the Church credit for condemning it, particularly as it was itself in the process of turning the historic Jesus into a "Lord" who sits "at the right hand of God." In the end, it amounted to the same thing. What Marcion tried to make of Jesus, a mere one hundred years after his death, the Church managed to catch up with in the end. Eventually it turned the itinerant preacher who regarded himself as a child of God into a God in his own right, thereby forming a mystical union with God and the Holy Spirit—something that an Orthodox Jew such as Rabbi

Jesus would have regarded as pure heresy. Jesus and Judaism knew: There was only one God, Yahwe, and no one else because, as it said in the Bible, he was a jealous God who permitted no other gods beside him.

Marcionism survived for a few hundred years on the periphery of the Mediterranean, but then disappeared. It is one of the ironies of history that the oldest preserved ecclesiastical inscription comes from a Marcionist church in Damascus.

Paulism, Gnosticism, and Marcionism—those are, from the viewpoint of Jesus, three heretic movements, three false teachings that turned what had originally existed, and had been originally meant, into their opposites.

But the Church never regarded Paul as a heretic, and when it turned against Gnosticism and Marcionism, it had already been infected by their ideas. Condemned or accepted, the Church absorbed the teachings of these three heretic trends and eventually made a good number of them its own. Some of these ideas can still be felt, while others have died off. But in one case the Church held on for too long to ideas that it had originally condemned, while ignoring the truth advocated by a heretic. His name was Montanus.

Montanism, named after its founder, was the first effort at a reformation in the young Church. It had the approval of the Roman bishop Eleutherus. Even the ecclesiastical teacher Iraenus traveled to Rome in order to support the new movement. One of the leading Fathers of the Church, Tertullian, who was born between 150 and 160, at first opposed the concepts of Montanus but then became one of the most prominent members of his movement.

· Despite all this, Montanism was later banned as heretical, and even today there are Church historians, such as Henri Daniel-Rops, who regard it simply as "madness." It so happens that this particular madness is nearly completely identical with Christianity in its earliest form.

In contrast to Marcion, Montanus, who was born in Asia Minor, sought close links between Christianity and Judaism. He emphasized the original Christian gifts of prophecy and ecstatic revelation. His favorite reference was a passage in John's Gospel that said specifically that prophecy would continue, even after the death of Rabbi Jesus. It is the passage that speaks of a "counselor" (Greek: *Paraclét*, also "consoler" or "comforter") who is to complete Jesus' revelation at a later time: "And when he comes he will convince the world of sin and of righteousness and of judgment. . . . I have yet many things to say to you, but you cannot bear them now. When the Spirit of truth comes, he will guide you into all the truth; for he will not speak on his own authority, but whatever he hears he will speak, and he will declare to you the things that are to come." (John 16:8, 12–13)

Montanus and his supporters believed that the voice of the "counselor" spoke through them. They called themselves "the prophets." As was done during the time of Paul, they experienced revelations they had received from the *Paraclét*; their teaching was not coagulated tradition but a "Spirit of truth."

With them, prophecy once again occupied the place it had previously held in religious service and congregational leadership. They awakened the memories of a "common priesthood" of the past, which the ecclesiastical hierarchy had shunted aside long ago.

Montanism was a break toward a vital Christianity at a time when the movement, barely a hundred years old, had already grown torpid and bogged down in "sin." It was of the Christians of his day that Tertullian wrote when he charged that "Your God is your belly, your intestines your Temple, your circumference your altar, your cook is your priest, herbs are your charisma, and your belch is your prophecy."

It seemed time for the *Paraclét* to open the world's eyes on the subject of sin. The Montanists therefore advocated the strictest possible morality, including asceticism and readiness for martyrdom—something the Montanists virtually yearned for. Instead of hiding from their persecutors, they volunteered to suffer for Christ as Christ had suffered for them. They exaggerated and misunderstood a great deal—such as the rules of fasting and denial of sexuality—and were accused of romantic fanaticism. But this accusation does not explain the Church's reversal, which suddenly attacked what it had only just approved. Strict morality might be a nuisance, but it wasn't dangerous.

The Church was probably disturbed by the ecstatic element in Montanism, which introduced unrest within a Church that had only just settled down. The Church may have felt that movements which put prophecy above order and law can easily give the impression of anarchy, and that the fanaticism of pietistic enthusiasts is just a few steps removed from that sort of thing. The thought that devoutness need not be linked to law was still alive in the year 200, although increasing dogmatization had doubtlessly weakened its strength.

It would be an oversimplification to explain it all by saying that the Christians of 200 wanted nothing further to do with the original Christian elements of enthusiasm and strength. They had been promised a *Paraclét,* and Montanus had brought him; the prophets were at work, and men like Tertullian did not find this at all objectionable, since hardly anything the Montanists advocated went counter to the Gospels.

Why, then, was this revitalization of Christianity under fire? The rigorous ethics demanded by the Montanists were probably too much for the increasing number of Church followers, even though these ethics went back to Jesus. The hope for an early end of the world was probably also a factor in discrediting the Montanists. Karlheinz Deschner, in his critical Church history *Abermals krähte der Hahn (Once More, the Rooster Crowed,* 1962), has this to say:

"The most basic reason for Catholic opposition was probably the spiritual view of the church which the Montanists propounded. As the Montanists regarded themselves as the true spiritual church, they were a threat to the monarchic office of the Bishop. Montanism placed prophecy above bureaucracy, spirit above letter, enthusiasm above organization. By challenging Montanism, the Bishops were defending their personal positions of power."

The Church did not oppose Montanism because Montanism was wrong, but because it proved to be uncomfortable to the ecclesiastical hierachy. The Montanists were a reminder that Jesus had not envisioned either bishops or a hierarchy of office. The Kingdom of God needed no apparatus. It had been a long time since anyone had voiced doubts about the need for an intermediary between God and man. And the Montanists even created a church that existed without a hierarchy that took it upon itself to forgive sin or to represent God on earth.

The struggle against Montanism was long and drawn out. Montanism finally collapsed, three hundred years later, in Asia Minor. Justinian, the Christian emperor, helped history along by having the Montanists, together with their wives and children, burned to death in their houses of worship.

In crushing Montanism, the Church separated itself from its own past, because Montanism had been a repetition of the arch-Christianity of the time of Rabbi Jesus. Deschner summarizes this as follows:

"It shared prophecy, visions and eager anticipation with Jesus and his Apostles; it shared with the many church fathers chiliastic views, belief in a thousand years of rule on earth; strict asceticism can be found in the developing monastic movement. All features of early Montanism already exist in Christianity. This heretic movement which, as just about everyone agrees, attracted particularly the more devout, was simply the reaction of a more radical arch-Christian view against the increasing worldliness of the developing Catholic church. As Harnack notes, the Bishops discredited 'what was once precious to all of Christianity, because they no longer had any use for it.'"

There was one thing the Montanists had that the Church could use: readiness for martyrdom. It retained the power of office and gained the willingness to suffer proclaimed by the "heretic" Montanus; it was able to preach humility and assert power.

We will now talk about this desire for suffering before dealing with the one heretic who did not want to believe in a divine Jesus and to whom we are indebted for the Nicene Creed.

14

SEARCH FOR SUFFERING

CHRISTIANITY HAS the strange characteristic that it seeks suffering, instead of trying to avoid it. To a Christian, the idea of "bearing his Cross" is virtually a sign of identity. This began when Paul outlined the path of the "suffering Messiah," abbreviated the life of Jesus into a tale of deprivation, and turned it into a story of salvation. To follow in Christ's path meant to suffer with him, to die, and to be resurrected. Paul even bore the marks of the crucified on his body.

Paul's Christ, however, is no longer that of the historic Rabbi Jesus who wanted to live for his God; rather, he is a Christ whom Paul willed to die for God. If one eliminates the various prophecies and transfigurations of suffering and of the unexpected and unexplained death in the biblical accounts, Jesus does not emerge with any particular joy or understanding for suffering. On the contrary, the Gospels tell us that Jesus was in such fear of death at Gethsemane that "his sweat became like great drops of blood." He even asked God to "remove this cup" (Luke 22:42, 44) of fate; he felt forsaken by God at the very moment when, according to Paul, he saved mankind through his death.

Quite the opposite: Jesus healed the sick and relieved them

of their suffering. He did not fast like the others, and he was obviously not opposed to wine and joy; nothing shows this more clearly than the passage stating that Christ turned water into wine, an act that some Christians have viewed with embarrassment.

Any attempt at an *imitatio Christi,* to walk in Jesus' footsteps, might just as well have elements of an affirmation of life. Still, whenever young Christianity had a choice, it selected suffering (and preached heavenly joys).

Young Christianity battled Gnosticism, but it accepted its disdain of the body: The sooner the body is mortified, this prison of the soul is stifled, the better. When, in 250, the Babylon-born Mani proclaimed a dualistic concept of salvation once again with his Manichaeism, the Church attacked him. Still, Mani's asceticism and hostility toward the material world left a strong impact on the Church and managed to gain lasting ground. Whatever gave pleasure was suspect because it strengthened man's link with the earthly. To this day, the Church's sexual morality is an expression of this attitude.

Young Christianity battled Marcion and his teaching about a God of vengeance and a God of love; but his notion of asceticism, through which Christ abandoned the old body of the Creator-God, was acceptable. The Church condemned Montanus and his spiritual church, but adopted his martyrdom.

Since Paul, the Church has been susceptible to suffering. The "joyous message" or *eu-angelion* of the Gospels was perverted, through Paul, into instructions for suffering on earth. The joyous message of Jesus, that the Kingdom of God was to come in this life, was canceled and postponed for the next life.

And when the persecution began, the Christians already had a set attitude toward this experience. Its example was Stephen, the first martyr, who had been stoned before the

gates of Jerusalem. Christ was identical with suffering unto
death. The Montanists made a technique of this. When they
weren't persecuted and hunted down, they turned themselves
in, hoping that their voluntary martyrdom would lead to
eternal bliss.

The persecutions of Christians during the first three centuries did impose suffering upon them. If the Roman authorities had not hunted down the Christians because they refused to worship the image of the Emperor as a divinity,
there would have been no martyrs. The Church did not pursue
suffering, it was forced on it—that, at least, is one way to argue
this issue. But that does not explain why the Church clung to
suffering when the persecutions were a thing of the past.

Something very strange took place. At the very moment
the persecutions stopped, when Christianity became the state
religion, the first Christians moved into the desert, denounced
the world that was no longer hostile to them, and proceeded
to mortify themselves. Monasticism began. When others no
longer killed their bodies, they did it themselves.

Louis Bouyer, the French Church historian, writes that
monasticism was "an instinctive Christian reaction to a dubious,
although apparently justified, conciliation with the present,
based on the Emperor's conversion." He adds: "One has to
understand this reaction against the background of the Con-
stantinian Church which sought to make peace with the world.
Why the retreat into the monastery? Because to be a Christian
had meant, until Emperor Constantine's conversion, to risk
everything at all times: life, possession, work. After Constantine's conversion, one could be a Christian and still enjoy
all these things. Departure for the desert was a reply to this
latest seduction, this temptation by the world, by power, and
contemporary life."

St. Anthony, although certainly not the first but probably
the best-known ascetic, became the symbol of this other-

worldly, joyless, misunderstood Christianity. While Jesus could turn water into wine and eat with the publicans, the ascetics shook ashes on their food to make it taste bad. While Rabbi Jesus fed five thousand hungry people through his miracle of the loaves and fishes and with baskets of left-over food, an ascetic was regarded as too proud when he ate six instead of seven olives per day; he was chastising himself more than others who ate seven olives, but if he were to eat eight olives, he might commit the sin of gluttony.

Ascetics tortured themselves in order to kill off their sinful bodies. They stood in the unshaded sunlight of the desert and wove baskets, which they pulled apart during the night. They lived on top of pillars or in caves; they defied temptations; and the more they suffered, the more they mortified their bodies. Nothing, absolutely nothing, was supposed to give them pleasure. A single smile, and years of asceticism and self-denial would have been for nothing. They battled demons, and then as now, believed they were serving God.

Even today on Mount Athos, the Holy Mountain in Greece, there are hermit hovels, nests in granite, roofless and without water; nothing but hot, glowing rock in the midday heat of the Aegean somewhere between Heaven and earth. If a monk makes one misstep, no one will go looking for him because he is with his merciful God.

Why did Christianity go in search of suffering, and why did it turn suffering into a virtue? What good is suffering? It had, and has, to be good for something. After all, no one does anything from which he does not expect some sort of help or use.

When Tertullian addressed the antagonists of Christianity, he spoke of the Roman persecutions as having a missionary effect: "And yet, all your calculated cruelty will do you no good; instead, it serves to attract others to our community. The more you destroy us, the more numerous we become; the blood of Christ is seed."

He added:

"There are many among you who call for heroic endurance of pain and death. Cicero does so in the "Tusculanes," as does Seneca in his "Coincidences," and Diogenes, Pyrrho, and Callicinos as well. Still, their words do not find as many followers as do the Christians who teach by their example. The very stubborn tenacity of which you accuse us is our teaching. No one who witnesses it can fail to be aware of the essentials of our cause."

To Tertullian, suffering is witness and "sermon." Just as Christ suffered unjustly and thus changed the world, so did his successors suffer in order to make the world conscious of God's truth. And that is not all, because Tertullian says further: "If you judge us guilty, God will set us free."

Here, suddenly, the secret use of suffering becomes visible. Suffering helps to earn grace, to gain mercy. Suffering is a way to salvation. And now one can understand why Christianity was willing to abandon much, but never suffering. That explains, too, why the ascetics never freed their souls from the prison of their bodies in the most obvious way: by simply starving to death. Only mortification itself brings the desired rewards. Suffering on earth brings with it the right to celestial peace.

Actually, such a concept should never have arisen. According to Paul, Christ achieved forgiveness for man's sins once and for all. It is completely unnecessary and totally impossible that man can achieve his own pardon ever since sin came into the world with Adam, the first man: "If, through the sin of one only, many have died, then God's grace and gift have extravagantly affected a multitude through the mercy of one man, Jesus Christ. . . . If through the sin of one only, damnation can overcome all men, then the justness of one may be justification for the life of all men."

The unique character of the Paulist message was that, in contrast to all other mystery cults, one alone had served to conciliate all men with God. That was the difference between Paul and the Gnostics: not knowledge or insight, but a deed that had already been done achieved salvation.

The idea that man has to accumulate merits to achieve an additional degree of grace, through his own actions and suffering, is backsliding into what Paul had called "paganism."

Nevertheless, all this is psychologically understandable. Everyone has the need to be responsible for his own fate, at least to a degree. No one likes to be told that he is basically incapable of putting his things at least more or less in order. But that is precisely what Paulist teaching asserts: it puts the blame on man. He, never God, is responsible for all evil that may befall him, but he is apparently incapable of correcting his own mistakes. While man slithers into guilt, he has no chance of wiping it out because Christ has already done so in his stead.

Unconscious resistance opposes such a passive solution. No Christian will deny that Christ has saved him (although few will be able to say in plain language what this salvation has meant in their lives), but unconsciously everyone would like to vindicate himself. He would like at least a bit of help. Christ may have done the most decisive part, but no one is quite so passive and full of trust in God that he could leave it at that. So it is human nature to want to collect a few extra points— just to be on the safe side, and because it can't do any harm.

With that, Paul's teaching moved down to the level of plain psychology, which is where every religion finds itself when it involves man in his own salvation, whether that was the way it was originally planned or not. "Whoever strives with eagerness—he can be saved," said Johann Wolfgang von Goethe in *Faust*, a statement that, in view of the contradictions between dogma and practice, especially regarding salvation by faith or by good works, may well be applied to the Christian Church itself.

That is not the end of our exploration. I am still looking for an explanation as to why, exactly, suffering should be praiseworthy in the first place. It is certainly possible that man might conciliate God through positive, active work. The Sermon on the Mount provides ample material for such constructive activity. After all, man's sin is not simply that he exists—God created him to live—but that he has failed to live up to God's will and has thus incurred guilt. The commandments tell us what God's will is, and Jesus has repeated: "You shall love the Lord your God with all your heart, and with all your soul, and with all your mind. This is the great and first commandment. And a second is like it: You shall love your neighbor as yourself. On these two commandments depend all the law and the prophets." (Matt. 22:37, 40)

One need do no more than adhere to these two commandments, or at least try and adhere to them. They say nothing about suffering and fate, only about action, and Jesus taught no more than this and asked no more than this. For this reason, the Dutch Catechism of 1969 states: "Our God does not permit fatalism. Neither sin nor suffering have to be accepted as fated or respected as the Will of God. . . . The Christian is no less concerned with development on this earth than is the Humanist or the Marxist."

Rabbi Jesus did not teach us to be fatalistic. His path to God was love of one's neighbor, not suffering, as the later "theology of the Cross" falsely suggested. He also did not demand self-denial: We were supposed to love our neighbor—just as we love ourselves.

In reality, ever since Paul, Christianity has shown a yen for pessimism, which had nothing to do with the historic Jesus. Paul believed in predetermination of human fate. The dualistic systems that challenged Christianity in its younger years were all consumed with the notion of pessimism in a rotten world, with man no more than a ball being bounced around by principles of good and evil. Man was helpless and passive, at the mercy of forces greater than himself.

This feeling of helplessness is nothing new in the history of religion. The German Protestant theologian and philosopher Friedrich Schleiermacher called it the "feeling of unavoidable dependence," and used it to define the nature of religion generally.

This feeling of being dependent on outside forces is based on a pessimistic foundation, the idea that our own strength is insufficient to free ourselves. In the area of human dependency conditions, it is comparable to the idea of the slave who is completely subordinate to another's will and whose "sin" is a disobedience that is destined to be futile. This image of master and servant has left its lasting imprint on Christianity.

If a slave agrees with his master to effect a "conciliation," the active kind of neighborly love that Jesus meant, he is not likely to get anywhere. The master demands obedience, and nothing else. Obedience to the point of self-denial. Obedience also means deprivation. Psychoanalyst Erich Fromm writes in *Escape from Freedom:* "Frequently, this feeling is not conscious; often it is covered by compensatory feelings of eminence and perfection. However, if one only penetrates deeply enough into the unconscious dynamics of such a person, one finds these feelings without fail. The individual finds himself 'free' in the negative sense, that is, alone with his self and confronting an alienated, hostile world. In this situation, to quote a telling description of Dostoevski, in *The Brothers Karamazov,* he has 'no more pressing need than the one to find somebody to whom he can surrender, as quickly as possible, that gift of freedom which he, the unfortunate creature, was born with.' The frightened individual seeks for somebody or something to tie his self to; he cannot bear to be his own individual self any longer, and he tries frantically to get rid of it and to feel security again by the elimination of this burden: the self." A remarkable and disturbing expression of this self-denial through obedience that turns a man into a "lifeless corpse" can be found in the blind obedience of the Jesuits.

It is difficult to imagine a human being who would voluntarily abandon his own self. There has to be rebellion and some form of uprising and conflict. Such a conflict cannot last indefinitely. Either the slave frees himself and is no longer enslaved, or he has to adapt. Fromm writes: "As long as one struggles between feelings of power and independence on the one hand and feelings of inferiority and powerlessness on the other, there is painful conflict. But as soon as one moves the individual self toward zero and is aware of the separation of the individual, eliminating it, then the conflict is finished and one is saved."

A slave who denies his own wishes and his own nature, who wants only to obey his master, eliminates the conflict between himself and his master. The road to this is self-degradation and willingness to suffer. Whatever the master demands or orders has to be done or endured.

Of course, we no longer have slaves, and no one in our society is fundamentally compelled to deny his own identity.

The whole thing might sound like pure theory, but it isn't. Erich Fromm was not concerned with the psychology of Roman slaves. He described an emotional state that is frequent enough to be fairly common: "The most common form is the feeling of inferiority, helplessness and personal insignificance. These are not mere imaginings of actual neglect, personal slights and actual weakness (although these people usually explain them in these terms). These people have the tendency to belittle themselves, to appear so weak as to have no power whatever. Usually, they show dependence on external forces—

other people, institutions, or nature. They do not defend themselves; they don't do what they themselves want to do *themselves*, but obey the real or imagined orders of others. They are often unable to feel or say, 'I will,' or 'I am.' Life is something incredibly difficult for them, something they cannot cope with."

This Christian desire to subordinate oneself voluntarily to a Lord, and to serve him to the point of self-denial, belongs psychologically in the category of masochism, the self-torturing counterpart to sadism. And therefore, according to Fromm, Schleiermacher's definition of religion as an experience of absolute dependence is equivalent to "a general definition of masochism."

I want to make clear that this does not imply anything perverse, although it may indicate a tendency in that direction. But Fromm adds that "in extreme cases, of which there are a good number, one finds in these tendencies to belittle oneself and subordinate oneself to external forces another, parallel tendency to inflict pain and to make others suffer, which can take various forms," such as "to be overwhelmed by pain and suffering."

The ascetics, the self-torturing pleasure in suffering, the need for martyrdom, Paul's demand to bear the Cross (Paul, who specifically called himself "small")—all this bubbles to the surface easily and achieves meaning as part of a psychological evolution that is totally separate from the essential teaching of Jesus. The strange reversal of finding recognition instead of punishment in suffering has its beginning in man's helpless encounter with good and evil. This delight in suffering is more fully represented in the Letters of Paul than anywhere else in the Bible. Its hidden root is its pessimism toward a world order of master and slave; master, servant-slave, and obedience are the key concepts of Christian willingness to suffer.

And this is probably the clearest echo caused by Paul's

teaching: The downtrodden, caught within the existing and rigid framework of master and servant, were helped to understand their suffering in obedience and to transfigure it.

Paul's teaching of obedient suffering attracted the pessimistic elements of his time like a magnet. A teaching, originally designed to prepare for a divine kingdom through action and deed, had in three hundred years turned into a religion of blind trust in the Divine while hoping for Heaven.

Faith in God the Father had become faith in Christ the Lord. The community of the saved had become an institution of sinners. The child of God had become a slave-servant. Love of neighbor had become pity. Salvation had become mercy.

Faith in God became a teaching about Jesus, and the man Jesus became the Son of God.

Three hundred years of pious worship had been enough to make the truth uttered by one inspired into a handy religion, complete with book, confession, dogma, and instructions.

Three hundred years had been sufficient to transform man's direct contact with God into a remote effort, channeled through a Savior and institutionalized in a Church.

Less than three hundred years had passed since the death of Rabbi Jesus, and Christianity had arrived at an almost complete reversal of its original intentions. At precisely this moment, Christianity became a world religion.

IV

FROM CHURCH TO POWER

15

VICTORY AT THE MILVIAN BRIDGE

OFTEN IN history, when something unexpected happens we are told that a miracle has occurred. We are now going to deal with something that became legend, although in the Damascus experience of Paul it was called a vision and a revelation.

This is the story of a man of questionable origin. He believed in a cult of the sun, and it is due to him that the Christian day of rest retained the name "Sunday." Under the control and pressures exerted by this man, the first World Council, held at Nicaea, formulated a creed of Christian belief that remains valid to this day. Yet, this man had not been baptized and therefore was not even a Christian. He reversed the policies of the Roman Empire and made the hitherto persecuted Christian sect into the state religion of the *Imperium Romanum*. He was, of course, the Emperor Constantine.

The image that has come down to us is one of violent contradictions. Various historians have painted him in sharply contrasting colors. To Jacob Burckhardt he was "a cold and ruthless seeker after power," who killed his own son and—immediately after his return from the Council—had his wife strangled in her bath. This "Man of God" also had his brothers-in-law, Bassianus and Licinius, murdered to eliminate potential rivals or critics. Constantine called himself a bishop of the masses, and one German historian does see him as a lovable, honest, if somewhat impractical idealist. That is the view of Otto Seeck, expressed in his book *Geschichte des Untergangs der alten Welt* (*History of the Decline of the Old World*, 1895).

To some, he was a man of unusual, ice-cold intelligence, an egoist in the purple robe, who believed in total inner independence from all Christian sensitivity and who saw the Church as the only rival power of his army, who wanted the Church on his side and dealt with it accordingly. To others, he was a man who, despite his superstitions, arrived at a truly Christian outlook.

Some, such as Alois Dempf in *Geistesgeschichte der altchristlichen Kultur* (*A History of Ideas in the Culture of Ancient Christianity*), assert that he did not interfere in the problems of faith discussed at the Council of Nicaea, but limited himself to "appeals to peace and unity." Others, such as Loewenich, write that the bishops submitted only "under pressure exerted by the Emperor."

One group sees him as the First Christian Ruler by the Grace of God; others, going back to Dante, believe that the very establishment of an "Imperial Church" damaged Christianity's inner evolution and led to the dethroning of the Gospels.

These extremes of interpretation are no more than different readings of the same sources. Between them we can find, according to time and outlook, a variety of characterizations of Constantine the Great. The differences are particularly marked between secular historians and the history writers of the Church, who often keep silent where the others are outspoken. Church history still tends to maintain that what should not have happened, did not happen.

The story starts with his mother. There are still popular

Church accounts that create the impression that Constantine's mother, Helena, was a princess, and an English one at that. This makes a certain amount of sense because the Emperor's father, Constantinus (known, because of his unhealthy pallor, as "Chlorus the Green"), was one of four imperial governors in England. However, Constantine's birthplace, the former town of Naissus, is not to be found on a map of Britain because it is located outside Sofia, Bulgaria's capital, and is today called Nish.

The future Emperor Constantine was born on February 27, but his actual year of birth is not known. Estimates vary between 270 and 288; a particularly good guess seems to be 285. His mother was one of the "conquests" of Constantinus the Green. She ran an inn at Naissus; according to Ambrosius, this was a "Stabularia," a combination of overnight accommodations, stables, and tavern. Everyone agrees that she was, at least at the outset, a "concubine" of Constantinus. This is even acknowledged by Eusebius, who, as court biographer of Constantine, was not above outright lies when praising his master. It was left to the pious Middle Ages to find their relationship improper and to invent the English princess theory instead.

Yet, right there, in this little Balkan town, world history had its beginning. While Constantius Chlorus had three sons and three daughters by his official wife, Theodora, Constantine probably grew up with his mother. But the father-son relationship was not interrupted. Constantinus Chlorus remembered his first son and had him educated at the imperial court of Diocletian, who himself was born in Dioclea on the Dalmatian coast and retired to his birthplace after his abdication.

While staying with Diocletian, Constantine lived through the final persecution of the Christians. He fled, reached his father in Gaul, and accompanied him to England. There, following his father's death at York in 306, he was acclaimed emperor by his troops. Before his death, Constantinus who had always favored Constantine over his legitimate sons, had arranged his engagement to three-year-old Fausta, daughter of the Gallic Caesar Maximum. This was the Fausta who, when she reached the age of approximately thirty years, was strangled in her bath on orders of Constantine, who had made a certain Minerva his concubine. It was Minerva who gave birth to his son Crispus, whom Constantine in turn had killed later on.

The only one who survived this multiple carnage was his mother Helena, the Balkan innkeeper, whose sturdy peasant physique Constantine inherited. This energetic, no-nonsense woman managed, when Constantine was Emperor, to pinpoint instantly in Jerusalem the location of Golgotha. This was particularly notable, as it had been the target of many conscientious searches over a period of three hundred years. She even found the "authentic" Cross to go with it. And in Bethlehem, among hundreds of caves, Helena swooped down on precisely the one in which Mary had her baby. In each case Constantine had a church built above the newly discovered holy spot.

Helena remained not only alive, but also the recipient of many honors. Her son moved the capital of the Roman Empire to Byzantium, a good deal closer to home. He also named it after himself. With all his egocentric vitality, he postponed the fall of the Roman Empire by a thousand years. Today's Istanbul is merely a shortened version of the original Hellenic Constantinople. The Greek *is tin polin,* which means no more than "in the city," became Istanbul, a name that during the nineteenth century was further shortened, to "Stambul."

If Constantine had been born in the Britanno-Gallic region between York and Trier, if his mother had been Anglo-Saxon or Roman, all of world history, of Christianity and our own thoughts and actions, would have moved in quite different directions.

After being proclaimed "Augustus," Ruler of Gaul and Britain, Constantine began to conquer his own empire. Next to him, Licinius and Maximin governed in the Near East, and Maxentius in Italy. Constantine guarded the Rhine frontier against the Germanic armies and armed the Wall of Hadrian against the Picts and Scots. Next, he took a small army and marched on Maxentius. With North Italy in his hands, he moved toward Rome. Maxentius, following tradition, consulted an Oracle. The verdict was: "The enemy of Rome will perish." Maxentius took heart. He moved his troops up the Tiber and stationed them outside the gates of Rome. At the *Pons Mulvius*, the Milvian Bridge, he made his stand with his back to the river.

The decisive battle was fought on October 23, 312, and the enemy of Rome perished; his name: Maxentius. Oracles don't err, but one has to know how to interpret them correctly. The Roman troops were pushed into the raging river, and only a few men reached the bridge, among them Maxentius. The bridge collapsed, Maxentius drowned, and the victorious Constantine entered Rome. It is the old story of a courageous and a cowardly commander. History knows a thousand such tales.

There is also another version of the story, one that makes room for magic. According to this, Maxentius' troops are put to a rout by a fearful symbol with the powers of an evil eye. It's painted on the shields of Constantine's soldiers by the Emperor's orders, and they have God on their side. The awesome sign is like the letter "X" tilted sideways, and the "X" in Greek spells "CH" for Christ.

That makes the victory over Maxentius a Christian miracle, and Lactantius, Crispus's tutor, reports how it happened. During the night before the battle, a mysterious voice told Constantine in a dream that he should paint the initials of Christ on the soldiers' shields because *in hoc signo vinces,* under this divine sign he would be victorious. The divine advice was correct: With one stroke, Constantine became ruler of all the Occident.

Six months later he also defeated the two Near Eastern rulers and thus won what was known of the Orient as well.

He built an Arch of Triumph, the Arch of Constantine, in Rome, in which he also paid homage to Christ. Jointly with Licinius, whom he had killed afterward, Constantine issued the famous Milan Edict of Tolerance. Through it, Christianity was accepted by the men who three hundred years earlier had Jesus nailed to the Cross as a political rebel:

"Whereas I, Emperor Constantine, and I, Emperor Lincinius, have considered everything concerning the welfare and well-being of the State, we have decided among other generally useful edicts, or rather above all these, that, concerning the worship and service of the Deity, we shall leave it up to Christians and others which religion they wish to choose, so that the Divine Presence on its Heavenly Throne may show favor and grace to us and to all our subjects.

"We therefore deem it appropriate to order, with the purest and most just of intentions, that such freedom should be denied no one, whether they have accepted the Christian faith or whether they have chosen to turn to another religion they regard more appropriate, so that the Highest Deity, whose religion we serve freely, may offer us favor and general welfare."

Constantine became the first Christian ruler. Quickly, Bishop Eusebius of Caesarea, the Emperor's court biographer, reports that Constantine had assured him in lieu of an oath that Christ appeared to him that night, an illuminated cross in his hand. Eusebius had reported earlier that Constantine had called upon God and his Logos, the Savior Jesus Christ, for their support, and, lo and behold, just as God had done with Pharaoh in the Red Sea, the Tiber pulled Maxentius down into its depth.

That is certainly one way to write history. And to the present day, this is the way it is being told, varied and toned down depending on degrees of liberality. That is certainly true of versions designed to appeal to the uncritical masses, or, at any rate, it is presented in such a way that it does not antagonize legend-loving Christians, while critics are left to conclude what they like. There is no historic truth in any of this.

If one wants to get a detached perspective on Constantine and his attitude toward Christianity, it is wise not to rely too much on his hired apologist Eusebius. Jacob Burckhardt calls him "the most repulsive of all laudatory writers" and "the first utterly corrupt historian of antiquity." Even if one does not agree with this angry denunciation, it is quite obvious that Eusebius was always engaged in seeking to Christianize the Emperor's life story through retroactive falsification. Eusebius, stripped of his pretensions, was no different from the other paid panegyrics at the Emperor's court.

There are, however, other and more solid as well uncorruptible witnesses concerning the religious attitudes and beliefs of Emperor Constantine. These are the coins he had stamped, the Arch of Constantine, and the many sculptures he had erected.

Christian historians like to cite a statue showing Constantine with a cross, but they know it only from a secondhand description. The original is lost. There was probably nothing on it except the vexillum, the Roman insignia, which resembles a cross, just as the magical "X" on the shields could have been the Roman numeral 10, possibly used to celebrate the regime's tenth anniversary. Just as many tend to recognize Christian symbols where there are none, Karl Hönn in his biography *Konstantin der Grosse* (*Constantine the Great*, 1940) points out that Christian scholarship "began, a few years after the battle at Ponte Molle, to reinterpret cautiously the legends surrounding the victory over Licinius, as well as Constantine's actually carefully neutral religious approach, in a Christian framework."

This has led to the "discovery," where there aren't any, of Christian symbols in the Arch of Constantine in Rome, while failing to interpret what is really to be seen. What we do encounter is the symbol of the invincible sun god, Sol Invictus, which appears several times on the arch. At one point, the statuette of the son god is carried behind the goddess of victory; elsewhere, the picture of the sun god faces Constantine; then again, Constantine's head is surrounded by a circle of sun rays; at still another spot, the sun god drives toward heaven in a chariot.

Coincidence? Well, let's see. After the victory at the Milvian Bridge and at the time of the Edict of Tolerance at Milan, Constantine had new coinage made at Tarraco. It shows the goddess of victory accompanied by the sun god, Sol Invictus—exactly as they are displayed on the Arch of Constantine.

From the ancient city of Ilion, Constantine's robbers took a Porphyr pillar together with an image of the sun god. The emperor had it displayed in the Forum at Constantinople and dedicated it to himself (it is the so-called "burned pillar," which is still to be seen in Istanbul), and he was not at all disturbed that the pillar pictured the typical symbols of the sun god, the crown of rays and the globe.

Five years after the Council of Nicaea, the allegedly Christian ruler had himself pictured as a sun god. Only a single coin of the Emperor shows the Christ initials. It dates to about the time in Constantinople when the Emperor had, with pagan rites, changed his name; all other coins, without exception, show symbols of the old religion.

When the Council of 321 introduced the "Day of the Lord" as a national holy day, it followed the lead of the imperial chancellery and named it after the highest divinity, Dies Solis, Day of the Sun. Since then, Christians celebrate Sunday as their day of rest, not realizing that they are not worshiping on a Christian holiday, but are following an ancient sun cult. Even the cult of Mithras had known this worship of the sun, although Christians have done their best to Christianize it ret- roactively in hymns, and to sing that Christ is "the Sun of justice." When the date of Christ's birth was to be fixed in 358, the holy day of the sun god was chosen: December 25.

Constantine's cult of the sun had its roots deep in the history and mythology of mankind.

Amenhotep IV, husband of Nefretete, established the new religion of the sun cult, an early and exploratory form of mono- theism, long before the exodus of the Children of Israel from Egypt. It failed, and there were once again many gods. Moses left Egypt and had a vision on Mount Sinai. He saw a God who permitted no other gods beside him, and whom the Bible calls "Lord Zeboath," Lord of the heavenly host (armies). The Es- senes, whose spirit Jesus embraced, did not turn to the west, toward Jerusalem, as did the other Jews, but toward the east, toward sunrise. The Essenes spoke, as did the Persians, of the Sons of Light and Darkness, creating images that made their way into the New Testament.

These are not the only clues. The Druids of the north wor- shiped the sun. It divided the year into seasons, and it gave life. The ancient stone monuments of Stonehenge in England in- dicate similar sun-orientation. The strange, long-stemmed crosses in Normandy and on the Scottish islands, whose arms are wrapped in sun wreaths, bear witness of memories of the past.

Druids and the Mithra cult of the east; England and the Balkan cradle—Constantine knew both. But long before Con- stantine, monotheism, which Judaism embodied in Yahwe, had encountered similarities in the henotheism of the sun cults. Henotheism was a unique variation of monotheism. Here, too, a single deity—that is, the sun—was being worshiped, although other gods were known within the same religious system. Among these were Jupiter and Zeus. But the main god was wor- shiped as the only god because in the meantime, the Platonic idea of "a supreme principle" had gained general acceptance.

That is why the "Christian" Constantine and his apologists never mention a single Creator-God or speak of the Father of Christ. Instead, they refer only to a "supreme divinity" or the "supreme Creator of all things"—just as the "pagan" Licinius prayed before the battle: "Highest God, holy God, we beseech you. . . . Hear us, hark to our prayers."

They both had the same God in mind, but it was not the God of the Christians, and certainly not the God of Rabbi Jesus; it was Sol Invictus. Constantine makes no reference to Jesus or to Christ.

The bishops addressed Constantine as "beloved brother," and although he was unbaptized, he referred to himself as bishop and constructed churches and pagan temples simultaneously. He had himself baptized shortly before his death and was buried in the Apostolic Church in Constantinople among the monuments of the twelve Apostles as a thirteenth. This final Christian gesture of imperial arrogance proved clearly that he still knew essentially nothing *essential* about Christianity. Ernst Kornemann, in his *Weltgeschichte des Mittelmeerraumes* (*World History of the Mediterranean Region*), writes that "the thirteenth God, highly respected in antiquity, thus became the thirteenth apostle; this was still another weakening deviation from a traditional idea into a Christian pattern."

Constantine's motives remained obscure until the day of his death on May 22, 337. Kornemann believes that the "powerful activity" of Constantine the Great was "undoubtedly based on Christian theology." Joseph Vogt, in *Morgenland* (*Orient*, 1939) praises "his impressive Christian and Roman image in history," while Kornemann also credits him with a "liberating deed." Burckhardt sees him quite differently, and asserts that "the Christian Church could well have done without this horrible, although politically magnificent" figure standing astride a crossroad of history.

16

TEMPTATION AND RESISTANCE

EMPEROR CONSTANTINE created the Christian Occident. He lifted a minority into a position of respect and power. If it hadn't been for him, Christianity might never, or only much later, have ruled the world.

Estimates are that among fifty million people governed within the *Imperium Romanum* in the year 300, only about seven million were Christians; certainly not more than seventeen million. At the very best, they made up 30 percent of the total population. The Christians within the Roman Empire were, for the most part, poor folk who were scattered over a vast area and lived in many countries, without leadership or influence, persecuted by the state and ridiculed by the educated élite of Romans.

It is difficult to imagine why Constantine decided to advance this particular minority, unless he was himself a Christian. Why, after all, should a politician bent on power bother with a group that probably amounted to only a quarter of those he ruled or aspired to rule? But we have to get away from the idea that Constantine gave Christianity a boost. He simply tolerated it, together with other religions—no more and no less.

In the end, he decided that it would be advantageous to make use of it, as he had of other cults.

Constantine was a statesman and conqueror who put together an empire by many campaigns and battles (the political struggles have to be studied in detail if one wants to gain a comprehensive picture), and he had to try and keep this vast multistate ranging from Scotland to Asia Minor free of internal strife that might endanger its delicate fabric.

The Emperor had nothing to gain from keeping one-quarter of the population as his antagonists and to persecute it because it refused to bow down before the official symbols of divinity—particularly at a time when the silent majority no longer cared about them very much. In a letter to Anullinus, Constantine admitted quite openly what had prompted him to a new tolerance of the Christian sect: Disdain of Christian worship had created great dangers for the state, while its revival and maintenance had brought happiness and blessings. Eduard Schwartz, writing in the anthology *Meister der Politik* (*Masters of Statecraft*), passed this judgment:

"What leads Constantine to the Church is his skill as a statesman, not a pious heart. . . . The most important and most decisive factor in this decision was the organizational strength of the Church. The God with whom this Ruler decided to ally himself was not, as previously, the God of some pagan cult community who did not exclude other divinities, not of some loosely flowing grouping but that of a tightly formed, exclusive Church whose organization represented a force which the Emperor either had to break or turn into an ally, if his omnipotence was to be more than pure ambition."

The result was not a Christianization of the state, but the very opposite. Constantine the politician aimed at the nationalization of Christianity. Kornemann puts it this way:

"The most important achievement of his life was the incorporation of the previously opposed Christian Church into the

State itself. Like Augustus, he was definitely a politician of compromise, and like the creator of the Principat, it took him twenty-five years to reach the important aims of his existence: to fit the Church into the already transformed Augustinian State."

Burckhardt comments as follows:

"He attempted one of the most daring steps that could be imagined, something that more than one Imperator had envisaged but rejected: to separate the Empire from its old religion, which had reached such a degree of disintegration at the time that, despite the obligatory Emperor Cult, it could be of no use to governmental authority! . . . Although representing only a small minority within the whole pagan society, the Church was—if one ignores the Army—the only organized power within the Empire, while everything else was rubble. Constantine deserves eternal admiration for having foreseen the Church's strength as a future support of the Imperium, and to have treated it accordingly.

"In addition to his superior and ice-cold intelligence, and to his total internal independence of all Christian feeling, his decision called for extraordinary decisiveness and shrewdness. Constantine knew how to adapt his orders to the prevailing mood. To the very end, he was sufficiently strong-minded to offer paganism, simultaneously, defiance and a degree of benevolence."

Victors write the history books, and Christianity has quite naturally interpreted all this in its own favor. But Christianity has paid far too little attention to the oddity that those, who only just before had submitted themselves to martyrdom in order to resist divinization of the state, were now able to submit themselves to the Emperor. And all this while his panegyrists continued to shower him with divine attributes and, while he was building temples, permitted himself to be celebrated as the "deputy of Christ."

Christianity has not bothered sufficiently to wonder why all those whose existence was not of this world, were only too eager to seize power once it was offered to them. And next, in defiance of neighborly love, the persecuted quickly became the persecutors, who in the name of their faith killed many more people than did the Roman rulers during all their combined reigns.

Constantine's action, which moved Christianity into a position of power and turned it into an imperial state religion that permitted no contradiction, provided during the short span of three hundred years the final and most shocking spectacle of a falsification of its own past. None of this had anything whatever to do with the teaching and hopes of Rabbi Jesus.

It must now be told how, during this period and on orders of the Emperor, Jesus was made a God.

When, in the year 324 following his victory over Licinius, Constantine became master of the eastern part of the Roman Empire as well, a furious ecclesiastical battle had been going on in Alexandria for half a century. Several synods of the Church had already sought to deal with the drawn-out struggle between Bishop Alexander and the pastor of Alexandria's most influential church, the Church of Baucalis. One of the synods had found the pastor guilty of false teaching and exiled him from Egypt; the next Synod declared that he was right-thinking and faithful; and the third reinstated him as a pastor in Alexandria but did not solve the dispute.

Emperor Constantine, decisive as ever and determined to govern his Empire with a united Church, immediately wrote to the two feuding clergymen, urging them not to "cause themselves sleepless nights" over theological trivia and subtleties. But the quarrel continued as fiercely as ever.

What "Bishop" Constantine naïvely regarded as trivial was, in fact, one of the most decisive questions to confront Christianity.

The question was simply whether Christianity had only a single God, like the Judaism from which Jesus had emerged, or whether it had three. In other words, was Christianity still monotheistic as it had been at the time of Moses, or did it have a Pantheon along the lines of Hellenism? To put it more precisely: Was the itinerant Jewish preacher from Galilee a God or not?

According to the oldest sources of the New Testament, the Letters of Paul, Jesus was not a God. Paul is very clear about this. He spoke of Jesus as the "Son of God," which in those days meant nothing more than that a man had a special relationship with God. Rabbi Jesus never referred to himself as God; to a Jew, this would have been blasphemy. There was only one God, Yahwe, whom Jesus in childlike trust and love called *Abba*, or Daddy, the Creator of Heaven and earth.

There were, of course, certain key sentences in the Gospel according to John, the last of the Gospels and the one most deeply influenced by Hellenism. It said, for instance, "I and the Father are one" (John 10:3) and "He who has seen me has seen the Father" (John 14:9). Such sentences could be understood to mean that Jesus was God or part of God, provided one does not see them as part of a mystical union.

But one has to decide whether one is to follow the historic line that emerges from the monotheism of Judaism, or whether one sees greater truth in the Hellenistic influence on John's Gospel than in Jesus, who thought and spoke as a Jew.

The concept of the alleged Trinity, of a divine threesome, emerges quite obviously from the so-called "pagan" area and has nothing to do with Judaism. The religion of India knows such triple gods, just as the Greeks know of a principle of a holy three among their gods.

The early Church tried to fit itself into this pattern, and it melted Father, Son, and Holy Spirit into a three-in-one formula, which put an unbearable burden on simple logic. Still, Origen, leading theologian of the first three centuries, was still able to maintain that Christ was no more powerful than the Father but of lesser strength: "We teach this, because we believe in his own words, where he says, 'I go to the Father, because the Father is greater than I.'" Origen was referring to a passage in John (14:28).

But even here we see a hidden idea akin to polytheism, the concept of multiple gods. Theology was forced to take an increasing interest in the question of how the concept of a Trinity had to be understood, and what it meant for an understanding of the "Son of God."

It was a long quarrel. Condemnations succeeded one another. One side maintained its firm hold on monotheism and said that either Jesus had to have been God or, as there could only be one God, he must have been human. Others invented an "adopted Son of God." A third group tried a compromise and taught that Rabbi Jesus had been a part of God, but—as there was only one true God—had been created by God later on. And the fourth view was that if Christ was part of a Trinity, he had to be without beginning or end, just like God. In other words, Jesus was not a creation of God, but a special category of God Himself that had existed from the very beginning.

The argument was not new, but in the person of Arius, pastor of the Baucalis Church in Alexandria, it had found a unique and fascinating spokesman.

Arius was lean, of ascetic appearance, somewhat vain but well-mannered. Our sources say that he always made a strong impression on women. He was polite but eccentric, sensitive but capable of practical shrewdness. He was a poet and a propagandist of great conversational charm, who translated complicated theological ideas into popular military songs to get his ideas across to the masses. According to Schneider's history, the urchins of Alexandria would whistle one of Arius' popular songs, "Once he did not exist; and no one knew the Created One."

There it is, Arius' theology in the few words of a song, something people can comprehend. But for our purposes more background is necessary. The prevailing idea in Alexandria was that Christ had not been created by God, but originated with God himself, was a being equal to God or, in theological terms, inseparable and indivisible from God. Thus Bishop Alexander was able to say that Jesus did not evolve from a man into a God, but was a God who became man. As he put it: "He is a true God of a true God. . . . He did not, having been man, become God; but, having been God, became man."

After two thousand years of Christianity such a sentence does not sound strange. But compared to what the historic Jew Jesus taught and believed, this is incredible blasphemy. Never would, or could, a Jew regard himself as equal to God. Such an idea was only possible in Hellenism, where gods had intercourse with the earth, where the heroes of this earth could be transferred to Heaven and become planets like Jupiter and Mars. Such things were possible only in a society where emperors had themselves worshiped as gods.

The Church wasn't aware of this heresy at the time. The heresy certainly was not condemned. But in the year 321 Arius was condemned, because for him the man from Nazareth was not God but a man. "The Son does not have the attributes of God," Arius taught. "He does not resemble Him and is not of the same nature. By his very nature, the Father is different from his Son because He is without beginning."

In reality, Arius was still thinking like the earliest Christian evangelists, who spoke of the "Son of Man" when referring to Jesus as "Ben Adam." In the most original sense, Ben Adam does indeed mean Son of Man, because the first man of the Bible did not have a proper name. "Adam" is Hebrew for "man," just as "Eve" means "bearer." They were simply man and woman, nothing else—the very "Adam" whom Paul satanized because he brought sin into the world, and that sin could be overcome by no one but the "Son of Man."

Paulist theology, which from the beginning showed Hellenistic leanings, was able to turn Jesus into God, because the words "Son of God" were being taken literally, not just as the image of one graced by God.

Even Arius was not quite free of the concept of divinization, because he moved Jesus closer to God than to man. But he did feel that Christ is a creature of God, not himself God. Arius tells us: "Christ is limited in his knowledge, by nature subject to change." Which means that Christ is neither all-knowing like God, nor unchangeable—and thus he is not God but man. Arius insisted on this not for reasons rooted in philosophy or logic or because he had read the Bible differently from his contemporaries. He arrived at Christ's humanity because he realized that man can see his paragon only in another man, not in an abstract God. God does not lead to God. This can be done only by the God-inspired man, able to divine one world while experiencing life in the other.

It seems to me that Arius could have been the transition toward the original meaning of Jesus that was to be rediscovered under the accumulations of three hundred years of struggle and history. He still had a feel for the tender humanity of faith in contrast to the inexorable demands of theology, which, contrary to biblical texts, transformed a prophet into a God because a pagan environment wanted it that way.

Arius' was the last attempt, in a long chain of pious heretics, designed to protect Christianity from its ultimate falsification. His creed, which Jesus might well have endorsed, states: "We avow one God. He alone is unconceived, alone eternal, alone without beginning, alone immortal, alone wise, alone good, alone Lord, alone Justice of All." That is not a description of a Christ, the Judge of the World, still depicted in Eastern churches as the *Pantocrator,* the Almighty. Nor is it a description of an immortal Christ sitting "at the right hand of God," nor of a sinless Savior, because only God is completely good or has the wisdom to avoid evil. This is a description of the one and only God whom Moses proclaimed and whom Rabbi Jesus knew. And nothing, not even Jesus, can approach this God or can equal him. And not a word about "Christ."

Constantine, in a letter, called Arius everything from a "jailbird" to a "scarecrow," from a "callow deceiver" to a "shameless and useless figure of a man," a "fool" and a "half beast." The Emperor might just as well have used these epithets on the man from Nazareth.

Because of Arius and his numerous loyal followers who wished to return to the original Jesus, the Nicene Creed was formulated, and it is still being used today. It did not do much good that later assemblies of bishops restored Arius to his ecclesiastical post and reaffirmed his status. He died in one of the streets of Constantinople, the city created by the man who, in his ignorance, had Arius condemned at the First Council of Nicaea in order to assure stability within his Empire and to protect it from "theological trivia."

17

MAN INTO GOD

THE FIRST Council of Nicaea (today a Turkish town south-west of Istanbul on the Asia minor side) began on May 2, 325, barely six months after Emperor Constantine had tried vainly to bring the quarreling parties in Alexandria together. It was the largest assembly of its kind to be held anywhere in the Roman Empire.

The Emperor appeared in Byzantine pomp, and the paid panegyrists described it this way: "He glittered like an Angel of God within the fiery glow of his purple, the radiance of gold and precious stones. He surpassed everyone in his en-tourage in height, beauty and dignity. He went to the front row of the seats where, amidst the assembly, a golden chair had been readied for him."

Constantine gave a talk in which he called for peace and harmony. His peace-making method was simple. Any letters of complaint and argumentation were to be burned unopened so that "no one should gain knowledge of the argument among the priests." Although he did not act as chairman, the Emperor constantly intruded into the proceedings. It was his plan to abandon Arius, but to protect Alexander only up to a certain point.

The disagreement centered on a single letter in the alphabet, the letter "i."

Eusebius of Caesarea read a baptismal creed of his congregation that called Christ the first-born and only-born, who before all known time had been "conceived" by the Father. The bishops found themselves more or less in agreement with these definitions. But then the Emperor intervened and, to the surprise of the Council, demanded a brand-new definition. He mentioned a word that had not appeared before the Council, and it is not known who had suggested it to him. The word, *homousios* (pronounced "homo-usios") means that Christ is "of the same nature" as God, is himself a God.

This is exactly what Arius had been disputing. To him, Jesus had been the most outstanding of all creatures. To him, Rabbi Jesus was simply not of the "same nature" as God (*homousios*), but a creature of God although "similar" (*homoiusios*). (The second word is pronounced "homoi-usios.")

The difference that is contained actually and symbolically in this letter "i" put to the Council of Nicaea the question whether Christianity, despite all the changes it had undergone, was to remain loyal to Paul and the Gospels concerning the Messiah's humanity, or whether the process of alienation and falsification was to be continued further, making a God out of a man who had wanted to do no more than bring mankind to God.

It depended on this "i" whether the Church would at last cut all ties with the God in which Jesus had believed and with Judaism, of which he had been part, in order to say and believe something entirely different. The Council of Nicaea acceded to Constantine's demand: three hundred years after his death, it made the itinerant preacher from Galilee into a God, who was *homousios*—identical in nature with God.

Christianity at this point became an ideology, whose "faith" was no longer based on facts. It acted on its own and began to manipulate facts as theory demanded rather than having theory correspond to such facts, as had the teachings of Jesus.

And, as usual when ideology and power meet, the result was intolerance. This is what happened at Nicaea. Some six weeks after the Council opened, on June 19, 325, Emperor Constantine insisted that all bishops who had been present should endorse a new creed that confirmed Christ as God and condemned Arius. Anyone who did not sign this document was to be excommunicated and exiled.

Nearly all the participants signed, including those who had only recently been tortured during the persecutions of the Christians and whose scars Constantine had kissed at the opening of the council. Seventeen bishops sided with Arius, but only five of them actually refused to sign. The Emperor gave them time to reconsider, and another three decided to add their signatures. One of these was Eusebius of Caesarea, whose confession of faith, although decisively revised, formed the basis of the Nicene Creed. He said later that he signed not because he believed in the new creed, but "to please the Emperor." The whole opportunistic performance showed that as soon as the Church had gained power and influence, dishonesty came into play, and the end was supposed to justify the means.

Only two of the three hundred bishops had the courage to defy the Emperor and to remain true to their conviction. I think their names are worth mentioning: Bishop Secundus of Ptolemais and Bishop Theonas of Marmarica. The two men were excommunicated and immediately exiled from Egypt and condemned. Their writings were burned, and anyone who retained them secretly was punished.

Emperor Constantine had achieved peace by uniting ecclesiastical and secular punishment for the first time. The victor at Nicaea was not the Church, but an Emperor who believed in the sun god as one of several deities, and who did not mind twisting Christianity to conform to his own ideas. It is tragic, however, that the Church bowed so quickly to please the Emperor, because, in reality, the quarrel at the Council of Nicaea was not yet over.

After the council, Emperor Constantine wrote to the community in Alexandria: "The agreement of the three hundred bishops is nothing less than God's own judgment." But it was divine judgment manipulated by an Emperor. Of the one thousand bishops within the Empire, he invited only three hundred, probably those who were expected to be the most malleable, and had them brought to the council in the imperial stage coaches. Most of these were from the just-conquered eastern territories. Only seven bishops had come from all of western Europe. Pope Sylvester in Rome did not go to Nicaea himself but sent two representatives.

But even Constantine was unable to make the text and the forcibly obtained signatures stick. Despite the condemnation of Arius, the internal struggle within the Church continued. Eastern bishops who had found it difficult to accept the Nicene Creed on "identical nature," began to reinterpret the word *homousios* in such a way that they might possibly agree with Arius. It was an attempt to reintroduce the "i" once again.

Arius also had supporters at the Imperial court. Constantine's sister interceded with the Emperor for the condemned man, as did his sister-in-law (whose son, the first pagan Emperor of the Christian Empire, was Julian Apostate, who considered Christianity ridiculous and tried to bring back the sun cult). As a result, Constantine wrote yet another letter to Arius. He denounced and threatened him all over again, but he also asked this "man with the heart of iron" to come to visit him, to have a heart-to-heart talk with the imperial "man of God."

Just as unexpected as the Emperor's letter was the reply. Arius submitted a new creed, the Emperor accepted it gracefully, and two years after Arius' condemnation, Constantine convened the Second Council of Nicaea in order to readmit Arius and his supporters into the Church. The same synod that had just condemned Arius did not welcome him and the two bishops. But this time Athanasius, the successor of Bishop Alexander of Alexandria, refused to recognize the reinstatement of Arius. Even when the Emperor visited him in person, Athanasius remained inflexible.

Meanwhile, the Emperor, having discovered how easy it was to circumvent synods, convened another one in the year 334 at Caesarea. This time, he planned to call Athanasius to account. The new synod was called together, and Athanasius was gently pressured to appear. He was found guilty, lost his bishop's chair, and was exiled north to Augusta Treverorum, the city later known as Trier.

Finally, more than ten years after the Council of Nicaea, the new synod at Jerusalem lifted the ban on Arius once and for all and resinstated him at this Alexandria post. The heretic against whom a new creed had been formulated returned to the Church—perhaps because he gave in, perhaps because a compromise had been worked out with the others, perhaps because the sensitive man was broken and exhausted, too tired to continue the fight; or, maybe, because he and his followers still believed that it was possible to speak of Christ's humanity. I do not know.

Arius died before he had a chance to return to Egypt. His teaching continued to be fought by the Church, and his theories were suppressed. But his ideas never quite succumbed. As one Church historian, Bernhard Lohse, writes in *Motive im Glauben* (*Motivation for Belief*): "Arius reminds us that Jesus, as he is described in the Gospels, was not a God who walked this earth, but truly a human being. Of course, by his very humanity Jesus proved his full community with God."

Arius desired nothing else, but the Church chose a different road; as it had done so often, it condemned what was right and retained what was false. As so often before and since, it did not ask: What is to be? As so often before and since, it did not ask what is true, but: Will it be useful? As so often before and since, it forgot what Jesus really believed and had sought to accomplish. And so it condemned Arius but fashioned a creed to accommodate an Emperor who still believed in the god of light, a creed that retains its validity to this day:

"We believe in one God, the almighty Father, the Creator of all that is Visible and Invisible, and in one Lord Jesus Christ, the Son of God, the First-Born who was conceived by his Father [i.e., from the essence of the Father] God from God, Light of Light, true God from true God, conceived and not created, identical in nature [*homousios*] with the Father. Through him, all has become, what exists in Heaven and on Earth, who, for us men and for our salvation, came down and became flesh, became man, suffered and on the third day was risen and went to Heaven, and who will return to judge the living and the dead; and in the Holy Spirit."

Jesus the Jew would have to remain silent, or perhaps would have protested, in the face of all these politicotheological theatrics. To him, what was here attributed to Christ and the Messiah was pure blasphemy. The Nicene Creed has a supplement, which reads as follows:

"As for those who say, 'There was a time when he was not,' and 'before he was begotten, he was not,' and 'he was made from that which was not, or from another hypostasis or substance,' or 'the Son of God is created, changeable and mutable,' there the Catholic Church anathemizes."

At this point, Rabbi Jesus, the man from Galilee, would have to shake his head and say: What was I except a man in search of God, the only God, the almighty Father, Creator of all that is Visible and Invisible? Mary, my mother, conceived me and bore me, as millions of mothers conceive and bear their children. I have sought God, as have millions of others, and I thought that I had found him, found this shelter with a Father who protects, helps, and forgives. I was killed, and I despaired in God, as have millions who perish before their lives are completed. I know the feeling of having been abandoned by God, as do many others, except that I admitted it. I was a man like all the others. I wept when Lazarus died. I liked the rich young man, and I have loved and hated people. I was rude to my mother and kindly to strangers. And I knew that no one is without sin except God alone.

And then this man would have to withdraw and wait. Because the Church, which asserts that it proclaims him, has obscured and distorted his person. It specifically condemned it with the Nicene Creed; it did not want to believe *with* Jesus, but *in* him.

V

FROM POWER TO IDEOLOGY

18

LOSS OF REALITY

THIS REPORT on the Church is now complete. Just as man's character is formed during childhood and merely grows along the same lines in later life, so did the Church develop its characteristics in its early centuries, once and for all. Today, the Church is what it became then; the more it gained in organization, the more it abandoned its original belief.

After Jesus' death, Paul turned faith into a teaching. Instead of the Kingdom of God, the Church appeared, and at the first opportunity it signed a pact with worldly power. It was not restrained by the biblical traditions or by Jesus' saying that his Kingdom was not of this world. Teaching and dogma took on a life of their own. After less than three hundred years, the preacher of penitence had become a Savior; the Son of Man was transformed into a God. What had been so fondly described as the highest commandment, the love of one's neighbor, was pushed into the ghetto of ministering to the poor. The unique commandment to love one's enemy became a prayer that was uttered while arms were blessed with which to murder the enemies of Christianity.

Ideals and reality grew farther apart. Historical truth and faith had less and less in common. What had long been in preparation became reality with Constantine's interference. As faith spread through the power of worldly strength, historical reality became unimportant, because he who has the power can impose his own truths. Constantine proved this, and Church history offers many examples of power-conscious disdain—up to, and including, the bodily ascension of Mary to heaven, which became reality and truth through the decree of dogma without the slightest hint of historical documentation or even a single, clear-cut indication in the Bible. This act imposed a change on Roman Catholic belief in one day.

I have been interested from the start in the question of how a religion develops, how it seeks to formulate an answer, and in the questions that everyone puts at least once: where do we come from? What are we here for? Where are we going? I have traced this question in Christianity because it is the single most powerful force that formed our thoughts and feelings for nearly two thousand years, whether or not we call ourselves Christians.

I wonder whether the historic development of Christianity was inevitable, whether things would have come out the way they did, no matter what.

For a moment we should re-examine the Church as we would the various phases in the lifespan of a man, although I am aware that human life cannot be projected, phase by phase, on the history of something superindividual, such as whole nations.

Perhaps the later development of Christianity was conditioned by its beginning in the Palestinian environment, where it lacked the sheltered protection and welfare of a cordial society. Even before it became fully conscious of its own identity, Jesus' belief moved like a foundling into the alien Greek surroundings. Once there, it was formed by men who actually knew nothing of its original setting; they were unaware of the child's inner tendencies but proceeded to force the foundling into a pattern with which they were familiar and that *they* regarded as correct.

At times—but much too rarely—old dreamlike memories come to the surface. They were elusive, hazy, but filled with yearning for the very beginning, when everything was still as it should be, when tradition and environment were one. These are moments of truth. Quickly, and much too often, they are suppressed by the life pattern of the foster parents, who should have been loving parents but understood nothing but themselves.

This might be one explanation of why Christianity, young and full of trusting innocence, went along with the bad guy who pretended to care about the child who had been battered and pushed around, and who gave him a taste of the candy of power.

This might help to explain why the Church in later life, despite all its increasing power, remained so touchy and defensive, forever musing about itself. It never did get over its childhood experiences. Whether it likes it or not, the Church spent two thousand years wrestling with the trauma of an orphan who had learned to juggle caution and love. During brief moments of forgetting, during a temporary euphoria, it called itself *ecclesia triumphans,* Church Victorious. Those were the days when it had the unconcerned flair of a very young man who sets out to conquer the world with the self-centered single-mindedness that forces others to do things his way whether they like it or not.

Then came the transition of adolescence, alternating between childhood and maturity, between a mystical and tortured self-examination and an alert observation of the world. Next came the reversals of puberty, the delight in abstract insights and flashes of brilliant intuition that dissect the world but do not quite grasp its totality. That was when Thomas Aquinas dealt for the first time with the logic of reality.

And next, the arrogance that is rooted in pure theory and tries to make reality conform to it, simply because a preconceived pattern demands it. That is an echo of Augustine, who called for a divine state in Carthage while the Vandals were sacking Rome.

Beyond this lies the insolence that forced King Henry IV to make his demeaning pilgrimage to Canossa to retain his throne; and there was the satiated power of the Church, which suddenly discovered that worldly power did not lead to God and which once again sought a merciful God, if not a merciful Church. Through Luther, the Church managed to grope toward maturity, even though the Roman Catholic Church did not care to admit this; it had the habit of rigid traditionalists of contradicting all challenging ideas, whether or not the arguments are truly valid.

But every revolution yearns for palaces. Even Luther had a weakness for nobility. During a peasant uprising, he took sides against the oppressed, and he was guilty—in retrospect more than in his own time—before the man from Nazareth, who two thousand years earlier favored those who labor and are heavy-laden. That is the case, I submit, even if one considers the desperate violations of human conduct of which the rebels of the time were guilty.

Both the Church of the Reformation and the Church of tradition grew as rigid as the once-revolutionary monastic orders in their attempts to regain the inspirations of the past. It is the tragic element, an essential part of history, that Christians were never able—from the very start—to free themselves of their early trauma, to develop without emotional fetters. The Church defends a past that does not really belong to it, and it just doesn't have the courage to express solidarity with its own beginning. If it did, too much might fall apart.

The Church has lived a life of alienation. Always in search of recognition, even if it meant using force. It has also been a life of intolerance. It has paid the price in truth, as when it promised free passage to Jan Hus but instead imprisoned the condemned heretic and burned him. The Church lived the life of a faith that was not really its own, no matter how loud its insistence. Instead it lived one that it had taken over from its powerful foster parents and that reflected the strong impressions gathered in childhood.

Was the history of Christianity dictated by a past with which it had never come to terms? Would this explain its rigidity, the uneasiness that showed itself most clearly when it should have met a new generation that doubted everything that had ever been assumed? This youthful privilege, which the Church itself had once demanded, should have been met with a sincere effort to explain and offer help during the vital period of the Enlightenment. Instead, the Church retaliated with the kind of panic that grips those who lack a natural authority that is accepted without questions. It behaved in the authoritarian manner of those who must pretend an authority they do not command.

Although these characteristics of a faith fascinate me, I should like to explore still another avenue of inquiry. It leads to a thought I should like to formulate in some detail. On the way to this new aspect, a game of dates and numbers attracts my attention. True, cold numbers mean nothing where life is involved, but they may give us a hint. Every figure that comes to mind represents development.

Rhythm is rarely fixed. Twelve hundred years before the beginning of the Christian era, Moses took the "chosen" people to Mount Sinai and presented them with the Ten Commandments of their God. Six hundred years before Christ, an Indian prince whom we know under the name of Buddha, the Enlightened One, finds salvation in the Wheel of Rebirth, linking salvation from guilt with detachment from all that is worldly.

Six hundred years later, a Jew in exile named Paul felt that not man but God himself is guilty. Not man but God must be the sacrifice that is necessary to wipe out Original Sin.

Some twenty generations and still another six hundred years later, the Prophet Mohammed came to the conclusion that neither man nor God, but fate, is the decisive force in the world; Kismet is unchangeable. Buddha was able to save himself; with Paul it was God who saved the world; Mohammed knew no salvation but only the fulfillment of a divine fate for better or worse.

Some six hundred years later still—about the year 1200—we find no date for a new idea that might have challenged the world. Perhaps it was suppressed by the power of Christianity, or, although it may be visible, we are not able to recognize it. Possibly, its breakthrough was delayed. There may have been something new, not clear at the time, in the Crusades, the philosophical abstractions of Aquinas, the discovery of the New World, or the Reformation.

Another six hundred years later, about 1800, within this rhythm, a man was born who saw the salvation of mankind in quite different terms: not in its detachment from this world, not in the extrasensory, in divine but arbitrary mercy, not in fate. Like the man of Nazareth, this nineteenth-century figure was concretely concerned with the here and now. He was the Jew Karl Marx, who dreamed of a changed world so that man might comprehend and experience his wherefrom, why, and whereto. He anticipated a paradise in this world, not in another, not in a great beyond. Not God's unchangeable laws, but the laws of capital and labor, he maintained, those of master and servant, decide the meaning of life. Not Buddhist negation of the world, not the fatalism of Islam, nor the humility of Christianity, but man's own activities are his fate.

Right or wrong, he put his thesis forward, and it has had its results in the history of human thought.

Let us, first of all, look at geography. Before this, all religions of the world came from the sub-tropical zones, which encourage passivity rather than decisive activity. Anyone who is familiar with southern regions can see this easily. Next, let us deal with the geographic flow of ideas and experiences. Three-hundred years after Buddha, the armies of Alexander the Great reached India. Legend has it that Aquinas did missionary work in India, and curiously, a thousand-year-old prayer recited by the monks on Mount Athos in Greece uses the breathing exercises of Indian yoga, but there are no clear historic links between these two events.

With Mohammed, a dependence on Christianity is still quite easy to detect. The Koran contains many Christian legends and stories. But time and again, Mohammed seeks to present Christianity as a mere preparation to "true insight." To him, Jesus was just one of the prophets who spoke of Allah.

Marx, on the other hand, lived with antithesis. He was opposed to a formal Christianity whose firm link with Empire and Emperor consequently appeared to him as "opium for the people"—a people, in fact, who could not differentiate between Emperor and God, and had resigned themselves to both instead of helping themselves.

With all due inhibitions that may affect me as a descendant of the "Christian Occident," the starting points of Jesus and Marx seem closer than all others. Jesus, through everything he put forward, envisaged a paradise beyond as little as did Marx. They had the same aim in mind despite different viewpoints. They sought perfection on earth: "Thy kingdom come, on earth as it is in Heaven." Both believed in earthly changes based on human action. They advocated self-assertion rather than passivity: Love thy neighbor as thyself. They know that a camel is more likely to go through a needle's eye than a rich man to enter the Kingdom of Heaven. As Jews, both knew that the just do not reach "bliss" or salvation from evil through mere "faith" but through deeds.

Of course, one is faith and the other is ideology. That is the basic difference: Faith is independent of proof in the world's reality; ideology is not.

That is as far as we may take this game of numbers, which leads us through various phases of history up to the present. It gives us a rhythm for the aging of the Church, and the interrelationship among ideas which, each in its turn, comes to life, grows, matures and fades with age.

Strangely enough, none of these religions has died out, as, for example, the Greek Pantheon did. Where they met, they battled one another, but they remained intact, and that goes for ancient Buddhism as much as for the relatively young Islam. But they changed as soon as they had become established and linked with power. Buddha, who knew no God, became himself a God. The everpresent Yahwe, who communicated to David, "I have not dwelt in a house" (II Sam. 7:6), evolved under David's son King Solomon into a domesticated God for whom a temple was built in the capital city of Jerusalem. And Christianity, too, taught and did after three hundred years very nearly the opposite of what Jesus had sought.

All these changes point in the same direction. New ideas gain in depth as long as they are concentrated in a limited circle; as soon as they expand and establish themselves, they grow shallow. If we wonder whether the development of Christianity has been unavoidable, we must remember that it is, after all, only one of many religions.

I also believe that during the process of aging and expansion, religions lose their original belief, and, without being aware of it, they become what they oppose: ideologies.

19

THE MANUFACTURED FAITH

THE NOTED theologian Klaus Scholder, writing in the Swiss newspaper *Basler Nationalzeitung* (March 9, 1969) about the confusing uses of the word "ideology," stated that the end of the eighteenth century brought France "a philosophical trend" designed to use what it called "ideas" or emotional elements for "practical techniques in education, ethics and politics." To do this, it sought to arrive at a "precise identification and description" of such "ideas." This concept was given the name "ideology." As the revolutionary government of that time acknowledged only this particular philosophy, people in France tended to call all philosophers "ideologists."

And then something important happened. Napoleon, under fire from the ideologists for his high-handed dictatorial manner, picked up the word and used it in a consistently derogatory manner. As Scholder reminds us, "he regarded anyone as an ideologist who had—in his sense, erroneous—relations to reality based on ideas."

This gave the concept of ideology a negative connotation, and that is the way Marx also used it. Scholder wrote that Marx spoke of middle-class views as an "ideology," meaning that it "ignored the realities of man and his world." The example of

Marx indicates that the derogatory label "ideology" was always applied by those who represented a particular social level. Whatever did not conform to the outlook of a governing society, and did not agree with its set of values, was seen as unrealistic and therefore ideological. To Marx, the bourgeoisie ignored reality, and to a capitalist, Marxism is a system that does not correspond to his value system and is to be denounced as an ideology.

We can speak of an ideology, therefore, only when a viewpoint or philosophical system is linked to a specific social group or level and aspires thereby to become politically effective or when it is politically effective. Ideology is always in search of political power. From the viewpoint of sociology, ideology is an aspiration to political rule, which it first seeks to obtain and then seeks to maintain with all available means.

What is confusing is that a governing ideology does not refer to itself as an ideology and tends to reject this epithet sharply. If it were to admit that it is an ideology, it would also admit that it is out of touch with reality, that it can only force reality to conform to its ideas. At the same time, it is constantly engaged in adjusing reality to ideas, rather than the other way around. Scholder wrote that "the only way to prove an opponent to be an ideologist, while one is oneself in possession of the truth, is to achieve coordination with reality. It is therefore characteristic of ideological action to use every possible means to force reality into the patterns of one's own thought. The reverse, to adjust one's thinking to reality, is not acceptable because it would reveal these thoughts to be wrong and one would be unmasked as an ideologist."

For this reason, governing levels of society and their ideology never regard uprisings and unrest as expressions of genuine public sentiment, but attribute them to agitation or manipulation by foreign agitators or other "outsiders." As an ideologist always maintains that he commands the sole truth, any challenge must come from outside. This is a worldwide phenomenon, and examples can easily be drawn from all segments of the political spectrum and all geographic areas in recent and current history.

Because ideologists are forever in danger of being unmasked by reality, they must constantly insist on adjusting reality to their thinking, even if it means using force. Scholder said that "if reality does not conform to theory, cunning and force have to be employed until it fits." A revolutionary ideologist has to offer provocative resistance, he writes, "until the police is forced to use its nightsticks in order to be able to proclaim triumphantly that the western world is governed by fascist elements." The marks of ideology, whatever its label, are force applied to reality, intolerance, and the claim to be the only custodian of truth.

No religion has escaped the process of ideologization. Christianity began to fall into this category when it allied itself with political power and became a state religion. The Church is almost like a human embryo, which during its growth passes through the various stages of human evolution. This is an evolution that leads from the belief of Moses by way of Buddha, Jesus, and Mohammed to the ideology of Karl Marx.

The foundations existed clearly enough. Paul, in contrast to Jesus, reintroduced the master-servant pattern and gave the new sect a sociological basis. Through Emperor Constantine, the Church gained the power to have its claims accepted; by going along with the worldly ruler, it fixed the values and standards of society. The rulers ruled by the grace of God, and the Church, even though it maintained it was the servant of all people, most certainly never was prone to identify with those who "labor and are heavily laden," such as the serfs of the Middle Ages or the industrial proletariat of a later age.

Christianity, which had once been the advocate of the lowly and despised, sided with ownership and the establishment. It became the establishment in its own right, taking dissidents to the flames of the stake.

The Church can certainly state quite correctly that it isn't today, and at least doesn't want to be today, what it was even a century ago. In most countries it is no longer a state religion, it must compete with other groups in a pluralistic society (although it still enjoys certain privileges), and it no longer participates in power as directly as before.

But all this does not prove that the Church has overcome its ideological way of thinking, which molded it during fifteen hundred years. In a dialogue on the subject in *Ideologie, Glaube und Wissen* (*Ideology, Belief and Knowledge*), psychotherapist Paul Matussek said that "the Church, since becoming a World Church, has taken on more and more ideological characteristics." He added: "That does not mean every believer is ideologized. But we find as part of the propagation of the faith and in the practice of proclamation definite aspects that are characteristic of ideology, not of faith. Among these are missionary work with the threat of force ('baptism' or 'death'), denunciation of deviationists, enforcement of the right faith by means of the often cruel Inquisition, dictation of the faith on the part of the Ruler (*cuius regio, eius religio*) or even bribery to insure faith. . . . The hierarchy of the Church is used to judging and passing judgment, and the higher its level, the more it is inclined to act judicially; considering the judgment of others begins to fade, and a certainty of possessing the truth leads psychologically to a position which is ready to regard any attack on itself as an attack on the truth."

One may reply to this argument that it deals with ideological methods, with certain intolerant practices that show human weakness; the nature of Christianity, its faith, need not be involved at all. It is at least possible to conclude that authoritarian and ideological behavior patterns do not of themselves, mean that the alleged faith is no more than an ideology.

But Matussek sees different motivations for faith, and writes: "The psychoanalyst regards ideology as a position which selects the content of a belief not because of its meaning, but in response to certain intrapsychic processes. That is the case whether the practitioner is a Christian of one or another denomination, an atheist, or a member of Jehovah's Witnesses."

Matussek cites this example: "Someone who regards eating meat as evil and harmful will avoid meat dishes, but not because of the factual nature of meat. Rather, he will express internal emotional responses in a way which projects subjective qualities on meat, prompting him to become a radical vegetarian."

A theologian might well say that every Christian probably brings motivations to his faith that do not belong to it, but that as a Christian he tries to be guided by biblical truth in order to obey the standards he finds "in Scripture" and is thus unable, in all honesty, to read things into it that aren't there.

Matussek counters that "ideological attitudes reflect an inner need and essentially an inability to make a decision concerning faith, so that the lack of genuine quality in such faith remains unrecognized by the faithful." This brings us to a point that permits us to prove conclusively that the Church, too, bends so-called "reality" of faith to fit ideological viewpoints rather than correcting beliefs in the light of actual biblical testimony.

The simplest example is the Roman Catholic Church's consistent assertion that Jesus had no brothers or sisters, although the New Testament speaks of them quite openly. It maintains, instead, that the word "brother" means "nephew." As facts must not interfere with theory, biblical reality is revised to fit belief rather than vice versa. That is pure ideology.

This correction is quite understandable. As, according to official belief, Jesus was born of a virgin, a believer may well assume that Mary throughout her life had nothing to do with

men. In other words, the Gospel writers must have *meant* nephews when they wrote brothers. The dogma of the Virgin
Birth can base itself on the clear-cut passage in Matthew, which
says, "Behold, a virgin shall conceive and bear a son." (Matt.
1:23) In the original Greek text, the word for "virgin" is
parthenos, and no one has yet suggested—analogous to the case
of Jesus' brothers—that it may not have meant virgin.

We are not even dealing with words used originally by Matthew. He actually quotes directly from the Old Testament and
the Prophet Isaiah (7:14). The Greek translation of the Old
Testament, the Septuagint, clearly uses the word for virgin at
this point. If one assumes that "Holy Scripture" is the norm
and truth of faith, a Christian finds it difficult to avoid belief
in the Virgin Birth, which Luke describes so vividly. Subse-
quent English translations have split on this point, and they
dramatize a lasting dispute.

The Hebrew original of Isaiah does not speak of a virgin,
but of a "young woman." The word used is not *betula,* which
would have meant virgin, but *alma,* which is equivalent to
young girl. The Septuagint made an error and translated *alma*
as virgin. That an error in translation became dogma is something one might overlook. When doctrinaire decisions were
originally made, no one bothered with textual critiques or a
study of original sources. The influence of Greek thought may
have prompted the natural assumption that whatever stood in
the widely used Septuagint was unassailable; at any rate, the
concept behind it was not alien to Greek tradition.

But we did not discover only yesterday that the early Bible
translations were wrong when they use the word "virgin" instead of "young woman." For centuries, churches of various
denominations were afraid to upset dogmatic tradition and take
proper notice of a mistake that badly needed correction. The
King James Version of the Bible, based on the Septuagint,
spoke of a "virgin." But the Revised Standard Version, which

updated more than three hundred phrases in the King James Version and utilized modern scholarship in the study of early Hebrew and Greek texts not available to the translators in King James' time, writes, "Behold, a young woman shall conceive . . ." It cautiously adds in a footnote, "Or, virgin." According to *Divry's Modern English-Greek and Greek-English Desk Dictionary*, contemporary Greek knows both meanings for *parthenos*, "virgin" as well as "maiden." The Parthenon of the Acropolis in Athens, literally, "Place of the Virgin," was dedicated to Athena, the virgin goddess. The Hellenic residue appears to have been more than linguistic.

Despite the fact that scholarship has established the validity of translations that speak of Mary as a "young woman," such translations still tend to be opposed among substantial elements in the Roman Catholic Church and in major Protestant denominations. Thus, the Church acts ideologically, twisting facts to fit its theory instead of basing declarations of faith on existing facts.

Of course, faith cannot be entirely based on fact. If we can prove everything factually, then we have no need for pure belief. But where faith can be traced back to historically documented fact, including genuine and originally valid passages in the Old Testament, opinion and belief should be adjusted rather than imposing meanings that did not and do not exist. This is not only relevant for single words; words are symptomatic and suggest that ideological glasses have warped the view of other matters as well.

The theory of the Virgin Birth in turn created the concept of Jesus' "nephews," as well as the idea that he was free of sin, that he was not really a man but a God, which further suggested that the "Mother of God," according to Catholic doctrine, was herself of Virgin Birth and ascended bodily to Heaven. All this strengthens the suspicion that other ecclesiastical-ideological statements have changed facts to correspond with the "pure truth" of theory.

B. Klappert, in his *Diskussion um Kreuz und Auferstehung* (*Discussion Concerning Cross and Resurrection*), summarize, the viewpoint of much conservative theology: "In all of the New Testament, and on all its levels, we find in varying images one consistent viewpoint, which is that Jesus' death on the Cross is God's action 'for our sake,' whereby he who was without sin took the place of the sinners."

The fact remains that this assertion cannot be proven. On the contrary, the oldest passages of the New Testament, those most likely to reflect Jesus' actual sayings, do not mention sacrificial death or Resurrection. His sayings, of which the Sermon on the Mount is a representative example, are largely teachings and instructions. Their main theme is the expected Kingdom of God and a call for penitence. Neither the Sermon on the Mount nor the parables speak of sacrifice and death, but of a need for revival as the road to God's Kingdom. The prayer he teaches his disciples makes no mention of sacrifice and Cross. Instead, all levels of the New Testament speak of a different kind of salvation, of "a baptism of repentance for the forgiveness of sins." (Mark 1:4) Sacrifical death wasn't even necessary and was not anticipated.

The numerous claims that Jesus' sacrificial death was a central Christian act of salvation or that man can only find salvation through Christ, who died on the Cross for all mankind and whom God wakened from the dead—to paraphrase some contemporary views—all reflect the "theology of the Cross," which the Christian Occident accepts as a matter of course because Paul offered this definition: "If Christ has not been raised, then our preaching is in vain and your faith is in vain . . . your faith is futile and you are still sinful." But Paul is suspect of being much less interested in the truth about Jesus than in his personal "intrapsychic processes," which prompted him to reinterpret the death of Jesus in order to eliminate his own difficulties of belief. The Jewish scholar Shalom Ben-Chorin writes in his biography of Paul that his tragic contribution was "the elimination of Jesus of Nazareth through his vertical [sic] Christ, with the result that little more than a theological abstraction remained which had a rather ghostly character: it was like the shadow of a vision."

Paul did not find his own salvation in reality, but in his personal vision, so that reality did not matter much to him. He arranged the world to fit his vision; he did not adjust his faith to historic reality. Paul, the first theologian, was also the first ideologist of the Church.

Church and theology did not retrace the steps that would have led them back to the living figure of the man from Nazareth who envisaged conciliation with God through the decency of individual living and who saw baptism as forgiveness of sin; instead, they followed the example of Paul, who manipulated reality until it fitted his own belief.

When Emperor Constantine came along and offered the Church new power, it was well prepared for imposing the pattern of its own outlook on the earth and to shape reality to fit its blueprint.

20

FAILURE OF A MISSION

EVER SINCE Constantine, the Church has been reading the Bible with the eyes of a ruler. But original Christianity had no use for the laws of power or production. Instead, it proclaimed an entirely different law. Marxist philosopher Vitezslav Gardavsky writes in *Hoffnung aus der Skepsis* (*Hope from Skepticism*): "The Christianity of the original Jewish community was critical of prevailing practical orientation and advanced this striking program: Not the Law of Power, but the Law of Love." When Christianity succumbed to power, all that changed. "It is possible to trace historically," Gardavsky continued, "how Christianity, after Constantine, began to yield to paganism and to the antique philosophies of Plato, Plotin, the Stoics, the Skeptics, and Aristotle."

He adds: "Viewed from the vantage point of the lifestyle and action of the Original Christian Community, the Church's later participation in power and particularly its own effort to achieve monopolistic control, are tragic errors."

The historic record shows a long and varied development, which presents the relationship between state and Church in the foreground while the picture loses depth and the background grows darker and darker. Soon, we can no longer recog-

nize that Jesus, who is always being cited, specifically disagreed
with the authority of his time, that he did not keep company
with the ruling establishment but preferred the alienated and
underprivileged. He talked of children rising against their parents and the sword, and challenged authority when he cleansed
the Temple. Soon forgotten was the fact that any claim to be a
Christ, a Messiah, meant in Jesus' time a change and overthrow
of existing conditions. Early on, the concept disappeared that
this Christ, whose name Christans adopted, had been executed
as a political criminal and agitator. The more political the
Church became, the more unpolitical it made its Savior.

The Church set its own standards. It regarded as divine will
whatever fitted the idea structures of the social levels it happened to favor. To be more specific: The dominant elements of
society created the framework, and the Church filled it with
Christian ideas. Whatever failed to fit this frame was simply
ignored, reinterpreted, or repressed, and it does not matter
whether this procedure was done consciously or unconsciously.

The poor and alienated were not forgotten, but the Church
viewed them from the position of their masters; it gave them
the leavings from the rich masters' table. But their fate was
not changed fundamentally. There were prayers for peace, but
also blessings for the arms of those who assured the Church's
position. It did not raise problems but traded in reassurance. It
preached against the violence of the serfs and the industrial
proletariat but forgot that the rulers had been the first to use
force. It recognized only one power as beneficial: the force
that took its own side.

Although the Church has lost much of its power and influence, little of its outdated routine thought has changed.
As before, it approves force when it originates with the ruling
levels of society, but denounces it when used by those on lower
levels. In Africa, when the Christian province of Biafra established its own government and split from non-Christian Nigeria,

the Church did everything legal—and some that was illegal—
to support Biafra. Moral appeals and humanitarian aid helped
to prolong a drawn-out war and the accompanying suffering until the insurrection collapsed politically. But when the World
Council of Churches requested humanitarian aid to African
resistance movements that fought authoritarian governments
and unjust racial discrimination, the Church quickly rediscovered the power of prayer and political abstention, which it
had practiced during the extermination of six million Jews.

The Church fearful of the concept of revolution, forgot that
it once rebelled against whole empires in order to bring Christianity to the Occident. Since then it has missed many an opportunity to take the side of those who labor and are heavy
laden. Whether the event was a peasant uprising in the Middle
Ages or the French Revolution, which we all acknowledge today
because our culture is indebted to its success; whether it was the
Industrial Revolution, or today's moral challenges to outdated
thought structures—all these have always found the Church on
the wrong side because it always stood on the side of power.

I am not even concerned with revolution as such, although
there now exists an impressive theology of revolution, but with
the question of how long the Church can cling to past structures that keep it ideologically imprisoned.

I cannot recall a single case when the Church called for a
boycott of the faithful—which would, at times, have been quite
possible—to halt or denounce a war. It was silent, at best, during
Hitler's war and in Vietnam. When it had the power, it acted
as Christ's successor only in hierarchical terms, but not in a living manner; and since it yielded power, it still fails to identify
itself unhesitatingly with those whom Jesus favored.

As before, the Church that proclaims the message of love
exhibits a preference for rule and power. Hans Bosse, a prominent theologian in the German Evangelical Church, wrote in
Die Angst vor dem Frieden (*Fear of Peace*) that ecclesiasti-

cal peace messages are "dictated by the conviction that the service of peace is a central component of Christian existence," but he admits: "The detached findings of the Canadian Peace Research Institute run contrary to this viewpoint." This is a reference to the institute's publication, *Ideology and Personality in War/Peace Attitudes*, by W. Eckardt and N. Z. Alcock. Bosse cites the Canadian study as stating that "particularly devout Christian members of specific denominations favor a tough line, a preventive policy which counts on the threat of obliteration of an antagonist. According to this, the devout fail to develop an initiative of their own that might lead to conciliation."

Eckardt and Alcock concern themselves with the question of how a Christian utilizes the help of his faith to solve internal conflicts; he seeks to find the nucleus of Christianity, independent of church attendance and denomination. The Canadian study concludes that religious conviction governs clearly visible attitudes and personal lifestyle in just about the same way as does a political ideology. The authors arrive at their findings as a result of a survey, which Bosse summarizes as follows:

"The main point of the Eckardt-Alcock study is this: Religious conviction shares one thing with nationalism, militarism, and conservatism: It puts its trust in force. . . . No matter how different various conflicts may be from one another, conservative, nationalistic, militaristic, and religious-oriented individuals fall back on the means of coercion and force. . . . It is disturbing that Christianity—the religion of love and mercy —appears to be linked to force, while the Canadian study finds that understanding and compassion for others is favored by non-Christians, as well as by those who advocate international understanding and social justice."

Not a Christian will to peace but Christian capacity for peace is, therefore, clearly in doubt, a condition that is the outgrowth of ideological ties to past structures.

Bosse observes, however: "The Churches did not invent force. They found it in existence and have participated in the long drawn-out effort to curb it. They have nevertheless contributed to an uncritical and hasty justification of force. . . . As long as Christianity is a Father Religion, not a Religion of Fraternity, this authoritarian attitude will remain."

The master-servant pattern of Paul, which separated man from God just as it put political rulers in the position of God-given authority, assured a reversal of original meaning, which has reached our society over a period of thousands of years.

The Church has identified itself with ruling establishments far beyond its existence, just as it accepted prevailing social morals, albeit with appropriate delays, as allegedly Christian. Lipstick and hemlines became criteria of Christ's succession, and the non-Christian cults contributed their antagonism toward the human body until it became a standard of Christian conjugal concepts. It is unnecessary to cite in detail what every one of us sees daily of the frustrating contradiction that different Churches seek to impose. I have sought to describe the beginnings of this development, which began with Saul of Tarsus and strayed farther and farther from its original path.

Ever since, the Church has presented Rabbi Jesus in the glittering purple vestments of divine power: Behold, thy Lord cometh.

And beware anyone who fails to recognize the lordly purple but merely sees a plain itinerant preacher from Galilee who took his God seriously, failed as Christ, as Messiah, and who died as an agitator on the Cross.

The Church remains in the condition we know from the fairy tale, "The Emperor's New Clothes." Everyone saw the fabulous new clothes, because they wanted to see them. But the Emperor was naked.

21

IS CHRISTIANITY DEAD?

NEARLY TWO THOUSAND years have passed since this religion was born. I am not disturbed by the mistakes and errors, the all-too-human aspects that are part of Church history. They are proof of humanity, and they do not disprove man's yearning for an unbroken "wholeness" of the wherefrom, thereto, and why that we call "holy" and find just as difficult to comprehend in our time as did those who were naïvely searching for it in times past.

Even though we know today that a genealogy of Christianity that leads back to *the* truth is only a human wish, not a reality, and certainly proves no claim whatever—we must nevertheless, I feel, acknowledge the tremendous influence of Christianity. We live off this Christian civilization.

Still, this cannot restrain our question of whether Christianity—despite its values—may not have outlived itself. Is it, like a white-haired old man, still dreaming of the strength of his youth, the successes in the best years of his life, not realizing that the world passed him by long ago and now has new questions that demand new answers? Perhaps Christianity has been placed into retirement by its own faithful who—aside from traditional family celebrations—have cut their contact with this institution, suspecting that the institution of the Church and Christian teaching have very little in common with the wishes of the man from Nazareth.

To this day, Church and theology have not overcome the trauma that the milieu of their childhood years impressed on their psyche. They do not explain or defend Jesus, but rather themselves and their salvation concepts. And these do not reach us directly from Jesus but from the Apostle Paul, who never laid eyes on Jesus and whom the first Christians in Jerusalem failed to accept.

Church and theology responded, from the very beginning, to the wrong stimuli. Like animals that respond to the key stimuli of prey and sex while shutting off all other perceptions, Church and theology respond only to their own key stimuli of words and phrases, to the exclusion of everything else. Paul taught the Church to respond to the stimulus words "Cross" "Resurrection." Regardless of what Church and theology mean by them, these words release in all theologians the identically strong, although varied, mixture of defense and rigid affirmation. Everything else may be subject to argument. Whether the miracles are true and veridical or not; whether miraculous birth and bodily ascent to Heaven are reality or symbol—all these are, except for ultraconservatives when questioned, merely peripheral.

But as soon as the stimulus words "Cross" "Resurrection" are spoken, theologians react like trained dogs to their master's whistle. They immediately assert that these concepts are the essence of Christianity, that they are the only means for man's conciliation with God.

Nevertheless, such formulas do not increase in validity simply by being repeated through thousands of years.

Actually, it is easy enough to imagine that our theologians might recognize the essentials of Christianity in something quite different, such as the absolute elements of neighborly love and human compassion, or the phrase that one can tell the tree of belief by the fruit it bears. Rabbi Jesus would have had no quarrel with any of these points.

The man from Nazareth answered quite clearly when he was asked about salvation, "Teacher, what shall I do to inherit eternl life?" Jesus replied, "You shall love the Lord your God with all your heart, and with all your soul, and with all your strength, and with all your mind; and your neighbor as yourself." That is the correct answer, Jesus said, and if you do this, you will live. (Luke 10:25, 28)

No more, and no less.

And here we have the essential tragedy: The man from Nazareth proclaimed the coming of the Kingdom of God; instead, there came the Church.

For the sake of the man from Nazareth, we should bid that Church goodbye. It actually had no use for him.

ADDITIONAL READING

ALLEGRO, J. M. *The Dead Sea Scrolls and the Origins of Christianity.* New York, 1957

BAKER, ARCHIBALD G. (ed.), *A Short History of Christianity.* Chicago, 1940.

BRANDON, S. G. F., *Religion in Ancient History.* New York, 1969.

CASE, SHIRLEY JACKSON, *Jesus Through the Centuries.* Chicago, 1932.

DAVIES, A. POWELL, *The First Christian.* New York, 1957.

ECKARDT, W. AND ALCOCK, N. Z., *Ideology and Personality in War/Peace Attitudes.* Oaksville, Ontario, 1967.

FROMM, ERICH, *Escape from Freedom.* New York, 1941/, 1969.

—— *Psychoanalysis and Religion.* New Haven, 1950.

HOENN, KARL, *Konstantin der Grosse.* Leipzig, 1940.

KLAUSNER, JOSEPH, *Jesus of Nazareth.* New York, 1953.

LEHMANN, JOHANNES, *Jesus Report.* Düsseldorf, 1970.

McCOWN, C. C., *The Search for the Real Jesus.* New York, 1940.

MEAD, G. R. S.,   *Fragments of a Faith Forgotten*. London, 1931.

OTTO, RUDOLF,   *The Idea of the Holy*. Oxford, 1923.

SCHONFIELD, HUGH H.,   *Those Incredible Christians*. New York, 1967.

SCHWEITZER, ALBERT,   *The Quest for the Historical Jesus*. New York, 1966.